THE AIR SHOW AT BRESCIA, 1909

The official poster of the Brescia Air Show.

THE AIR SHOW AT BRESCIA, 1909

PETER DEMETZ

Farrar, Straus and Giroux

NEW YORK

FARRAR, STRAUS AND GIROUX
19 UNION SQUARE WEST, NEW YORK 10003

Illustration credits appear on pages 251–52.

Library of Congress Cataloging-in-Publication Data
Demetz, Peter, 1922–
    The air show at Brescia, 1909 / Peter Demetz.
        p.   cm.
    Includes bibliographical references and index.
    ISBN 0-374-10259-7 (hc : alk. paper)
    1. Aeronautics—Italy—Brescia—Exhibitions—History.   I. Title.

TL506.I82 B733 2002
629.13'074'4526—dc21

                                                    2002023259

DESIGNED BY ROBERT C. OLSSON

www.fsgbooks.com

1 3 5 7 9 10 8 6 4 2

CONTENTS

PREFACE

Many years ago, let's say in the early fall of 1945, some of my former high-school friends returned from England to Prague in their dashing uniforms of the British Tank Corps or the Royal Air Force and immediately informed me that my views of literature were totally out of touch because I did not even know yet that Franz Kafka, whose father had a little shop on the Old Town Square, was the new and true giant of world literature. I knew of some of his novels because my aunt and uncle, on their escape from Berlin to Republican Spain, had dropped a few volumes on our bookshelves, but my father refused to believe that *der talentierte Kafka Franzl*, with whom he often talked at the corner of Celetná Street, was suddenly somebody like Dante or Goethe, and he insisted that my friend Ossie was simply exaggerating to impress the intelligent girls at the Café Slavia (as if his RAF battle dress were not enough). I had become a graduate student myself at the time, and began to roam the city to discover where Kafka had lived (his family moved every year with clockwork regularity, but always remained within the shadow of the Old Jewish Town), and I edited a little volume, *Franz Kafka a Praha* (Franz Kafka and Prague), published in 1947, that included photographs, documents, and essays by various learned hands. It did not have a long shelf life, as they say, because the new Communist government considered Kafka a "bourgeois existentialist" who did not share the constructive will of the working classes. Whatever the working classes felt, my publisher was forced to close shop, and few people came to know how proud I had been to unearth Kafka's article on "The Aeroplanes in Brescia" in an old volume of the *Bohemia*. It was important, I thought, to remind his readership that even the new giant of world literature started out with a modest newspaper article, to be read over breakfast.

The magic name of Brescia strangely impressed itself on my mind, and its lights flashed again when I studied the Italian Futurists and their avant-garde interest in early aviation. I thought of Kafka and Italy (admittedly a paradoxical combination) especially when I found out that Gabriele d'Annunzio, a Futurist in his life rather than in his writings, hurried to the Brescia air show of 1909, too, because he wanted to fly, no matter what, with Blériot, Curtiss, or his Italian compatriot Calderara. Unfortunately, Kafka and his friends, who had arrived there in time to see him around the hangars, had to leave and could not observe the grand poet aloft, while the Italian public applauded loudly. I was struck by the disproportions of the coincidence: Kafka in the cheap two-lire enclosure, d'Annunzio walking with the celebrities.

And so it happened that I one day found myself in the Brescia Biblioteca Queriniana, a magnificent late-Renaissance palace, to read microfilms of old city newspapers. I also walked along the roads, along the flat landscape where the air show once took place, halfway between Brescia and the town of Montichiari, and sipped my cappuccino at the Fascia d'Oro trattoria, once a small hotel where the first aviators had stayed when they came to the airfield and the hangars were not yet ready for their flying machines. By chance, I found my way to a simple monument to commemorate the aviation pioneers of 1909, almost hidden behind a little chapel and surrounded by tufts of grass and a few stone benches. Huge trucks roared along the nearby Brescia-Mantua road, and I sat on one of the stone benches and contemplated the scene.

I have to confess that I think of the present volume as an "entertainment," to borrow Graham Greene's term, not as a scholarly monograph, which I gladly leave to somebody else. I am intrigued by the Brescia air show as a unique encounter of resourceful engineers, daring pilots, visionaries from the provinces, and eminent artists and writers, and I should like to look at singular people and their special flying machines, including a few monstrous contraptions, rather than abandon myself to bleak generalizations. When studious Ninotchka, in one of the musical versions of the old movie, asks her American admirer (who happens to be Fred Astaire) about his theory of love and life, he responds that there is no such theory; and though I believe that any latter-day Ninotchka, trained at elite American graduate schools rather than in Moscow, would immediately say that to have no theory was a theory in itself (and a terrible one at that), I would rather side on this particular occasion with Fred Astaire and stay attuned to a productive chaos of details. I have convinced myself that the way in which I try to arrange my recalcitrant stories ultimately derives from my fuzzy memories of Thornton Wilder's *The Bridge of San Luis Rey*. I have to deal with more than five characters, of course, and yet I resemble Brother Juniper (unfrocked) who wants to investigate the lives of his characters before a pivotal event, and more; I would like to know what happened to my characters in later years, too, for better or, sometimes, much worse.

I am greatly indebted, for support and advice, to many friends and institutions, here and in Europe, and I wish to express my gratitude, above all, to Moira Piantoni (Brescia), who provided me with bibliographical data and copies of rare materials from the civic library of her hometown and extended her welcome hospitality to Paola and me when we went to visit the historical sites. Ludovico Calderara (Rome), son of Mario and formerly teaching in New York, readily made available to me his wonderful aviation book, fresh from the presses, and answered all my questions on the telephone; Giovanna Gambarota (Trento) persuaded a friendly publisher to send me a precious publication almost overnight, and my cousin Peter Brod (BBC Prague) and the historian Dr. Toman Brod promptly responded to my queries concerning Otto Brod, Max's brother and Kafka's friend. I was happy to enjoy encouragement and assistance at the Brescia libraries, the New York Public Library, and the Interlibrary Loan Office of the Sterling Library at Yale, and I think of my visit to Il Vittoriale degli Italiani (Gardone), the seat of the D'Annunzio Foundation, with great pleasure. When writing and preparing my manuscript, I relied once again, and with good reason, on the advice and wisdom of William B. Goodman, my agent, and I gladly followed the inventive suggestions of Suzanne Gray Kelley, once more my first American reader, who watched my prepositions and my syntax. I was happy to work on the illustrations with Luba Rasine-Ortoleva, my favorite graphic designer, and on the final text with Michael Schmelzle, now of Trinity College (Hartford). I am delighted to say how much I owe to my wife, Paola, when it comes to things Italian, and not only those, and how greatly I appreciated her willingness to suspend her studies of eighteenth-century Italian language philosophy, a problem certainly more lofty than mine, and to join me on one of my trips to the scene of the air show. The photographs of the historic trattoria and of the little monument to the pioneers of 1909 are hers.

New Haven, Connecticut
15 August 2001

THE AIR SHOW AT BRESCIA, 1909

CHAPTER ONE

Three Friends, Vacationing

IN LATE AUGUST 1909, three Prague friends in their twenties, and of more or less similar literary and artistic interests, thought of going together on a brief vacation. They wanted to escape from their gray old city and their office routines and stay for a few days at Riva, on the north shore of Lake Garda, the last outpost of the Austro-Hungarian monarchy and deep in Italian-language territory. The youngest of them, twenty-one-year-old Otto Brod, a bank trainee, had been there a year earlier and brought back glowing reports about the towering mountains, the sailboats on the glittering lake, the palm trees, and the celebrated people who gathered there. He had even met Heinrich Mann, less bourgeois than his brother Thomas, and together they had mailed a postcard to Prague showing Heinrich before the mast of a boat, with Otto in attendance as a kind of deck-hand, and Heinrich had written, "Nothing was more important to an artist than the admiration of the young who had not yet yielded to enthusiasm too often." Otto suggested to his twenty-five-year-old brother Max, a lawyer in the service of the Prague Central Post Office and a published writer known beyond his hometown, as well as to his friend the twenty-six-year-old Franz Kafka, who had begun to work for an insurance company, that they all go south together.

The brothers Brod had an easy time looking forward to the trip, for they had shared many vacations as children and teenagers, mostly at Misdroy, on the German shore of the Baltic Sea, the preferred watering spot of well-to-do Prague acculturated Jewish families at the turn of the century. Kafka, of a Jewish family of somewhat lower standing (his father, son of a kosher butcher, owned a reputable textile shop), had once accompanied a rich relative to the North Sea, but had never gone south of the Bohemian border. He felt a little anxious about imposing his presence on the two brothers and did not immediately make up his mind, but then apologized to Max in one of his frequent letters, saying, "If anybody had made such difficulties as I did yesterday, I would have thought twice before deciding whether to take him to Riva or not."

On Saturday, 4 September 1909, Kafka and Brod left Prague Central Station (Otto Brod was to follow immediately), and I assume that they took the fast train to Munich and switched there to the Innsbruck connection. Proceeding from Innsbruck over the Brenner Pass, they went to Bozen in the South Tyrol, in order to catch the train to Verona. The *Baedeker Travel Guide*, bible for all Austrian and German tourists, indicated that travelers had to change at the little station of Mori for a local connection to Riva, about twenty-five kilometers distant; and it is easy to imagine that the three young men, short on cash, paid one crown and sixty kreuzers each for a second-class ticket rather than three crowns and twenty kreuzers for first class. They traveled on that little train through a green valley to the lake of Loppio and from there up to a mountain pass, descending again toward the town of Torbole, and enjoyed a magnificent view of Lake Garda before reaching Riva.

At that time, Riva was a lively place of nearly eight thousand inhabitants, mostly busy in the modest tourist industry. (When I visited there recently, many tourist buses, most of them from places in former East Germany, were parking in the most improbable corners.) In 1909 there were about eight hotels and pensions (of fourteen) recommended especially by the *Baedeker*, the elegant Hotel Lido, Hotel Zur Sonne, and Hotel du Lac, but also a few simpler places like the See Villa or the Zentralhotel near the railway station. It was a tourist must to marvel at the Rocchetta, a steep rock crowned with a decrepit tower built in the distant past by the Venetians, and to admire the picturesque harbor square with arcades and an ancient tower with a clock. The sunny scene neatly impressed itself on Kafka's memory for a long time.

MY TRAVELOGUE, with its fast and slow trains, blue skies, picturesque rocks, and the lake, has been all too particular so far. But with Kafka, matters were, as usual, rather complicated, though not all difficulties were of his own making. The simple question was whether he would be allowed by his office superiors to take a vacation at all, even a brief one. Kafka had received his law degree on 18 June 1906, then worked for a while in the office of a Prague uncle, and continued on for a year as a court intern. But it was not easy for a young Jewish lawyer to find a suitable job. His family was concerned and turned to the "Madrid uncle," an almost mythic figure. (He was one of the directors of the Spanish railroad system and a man of many contacts.)

A job as *Aushilfskraft* (temporary assistant) was found at the Assicurazioni Generali of Trieste, a prominent Italian insurance company with a branch office in Prague. He had to work there eight to ten hours every day, was not paid for overtime, and was given the privilege of being permitted to apply for vacation time only after serving two full years. At the start, he felt elated, began to study a little Italian, and hoped the company would send him to Trieste for future training. After a few weeks in the office, located in the heart of the city at Wenceslas Square, his affair with an intelligent young woman of socialist leanings was going awry, and in the spring of 1908, young Kafka returned to his usual and lonely consolations in the night cafés and brothels. By late spring, his situation at the Assicurazioni had become untenable, and he had to mask his efforts to look for a job elsewhere. Fortunately, the father of one of his former schoolmates—an insurance manager of importance named Dr. Otto Příbram, president of the General Accident Insurance Company—made certain that a job was offered to the young lawyer. It was a meager position, though with excellent prospects, and Kafka accepted it immediately, making him the second Jew (not counting the president) among 250 employees. He was to work there loyally until 1922, when he was furloughed because of his grave illness.

Though he again started as a mere *Aushilfskraft*, Kafka's new job offered remarkable advantages to an employee who seriously wanted to get ahead in the insurance business and do his own writings, sorely neglected for quite a while. It was a job *"mit einfacher Frequenz,"* that is, office hours from 8:00 A.M. to 2:00 P.M., allowing Kafka to return home for an afternoon nap, to walk with his friends through the Prague streets or parks, and to work later on his own prose, if the mood was right (it seldom was). His superiors, especially Dr. Robert Marschner, liked him well enough, and sent the newcomer on factory inspection trips through the industrial regions of northern Bohemia. Quietly recognizing his literary intelligence, Dr. Marschner asked him to write technical analyses that were published regularly in the yearbook of the company; after eight months, his superiors praised his eminent loyalty and diligence, his commitment to his agenda, and his "literary talents."

Yet he was not content; he had not had a vacation for three years (his last he had spent at the Silesian mountain resort of Zuckmantel, where he found himself happily involved with an older woman), and he felt listless and chafed under the strict rules making him ineligible for vacation time. As early as 17 June 1909, he submitted a petition, on company stationery, claiming that he, for some time now, was suffering from a pathologically nervous condition that caused prolonged digestive problems and insomnia. On 18 August, now with the Riva plans in the air, he followed up with a certificate by a friendly physician confirming that Dr. Franz Kafka, after three long years without any vacation, "has begun to feel fatigued and nervous and to suffer from frequent headaches." From a purely medical point of view, it was necessary that the patient "take a holiday, even if only for a short while." The company behaved well. Forty-eight hours later, Kafka was notified (so much for the famous old Austrian bureaucracy) that his petition had been granted, and on 20 August he was informed that, by extraordinary permission of the director, he was free to take a requested vacation of eight days.

It does not seem that our three friends were too concerned with how short their vacation was actually to be, considering how long it would take them to get from Prague to Riva and return. They settled at the inexpensive Pension Bellevue, not listed by the *Baedeker* but close to the Rocchetta and with a nice view, spent a good deal of time hanging around the veranda, and went on an excursion to Castle Toblino. A rare photograph shows Otto and Franz, with floppy hats against the sun, rigging up a little boat, very *sportif* and yet curiously serious. Most of the time, I assume, they spent at the Bagni della Madonna under the Ponale Road, hewn into the rocks (it was less expensive than the bathing establishment at the Hotel Lido). Even after many years, Max Brod recalled "the long gray wooden boards in the sun . . . , the glistening lizards, the cool quietness of the place," and felt that they were really welcomed here by "the classic simplicity of the south," as the renowned eighteenth-century critic Winckelmann called it.

Between swims they liked to read, enjoying their little Italian, and the *Sentinella Bresciana*, the Italian daily published across the border. The issue of 9 September, to which Kafka later referred, immediately caught their interest. It would have been impossible, anyway, to ignore the headline splashed over page one: *La Prima Giornata del Circuito Aereo* (The First Day of the Air Show). As restless on vacation as he was at home, if not more so, Kafka immediately suggested to his friends that they all go to Brescia, Brod recalled, and since they had never seen any airplane in flight (though Brod had written an article on the famous French pilot Louis Blériot for a Berlin paper), they decided to go before it was too late. On the morning of 10 September they went by lake steamer to Desenzano, a trip of nearly five hours, making stops at Limone, Campione, Gargnano, Maderno, Gardone, Salò (which would be Mussolini's last stand), and Catullus's Sirmione. At Desenzano, they took the local train to Brescia Main Station, with its theatrical turrets and false crenellations. (They did not know that in the Austro-Italian war of 1859, Josef Rilke, father of their Prague fellow poet Rainer Maria Rilke, had been the commander of Brescia Castle.)

The three friends were having a good time together, kidding, laughing, walking, rowing, and swimming, but they did not show much interest in literary matters—seemingly. At the bathing establishment, they almost inevitably met and talked to the Tyrolean poet and nature apostle Carl Dallago, who quoted Nietzsche and Walt Whitman and, possibly, made a nuisance of himself. Max Brod testily remarked that Dallago "lived" (*hauste*) on the wooden planks of the Bagni, but his commit-

ment to an alternative way of life and to vegetarian nourish-
ment was tremendously interesting to Kafka, who later came to
read Dallago's contributions to the famous Innsbruck periodical
Der Brenner, which was also committed to the poetry of Georg
Trakl.

Max Brod had other plans; he had always been intensely involved in the literary affairs of his friends, especially if they did
not publish as much as he did; he interfered, cajoled, and wrote
endless letters of recommendation. He had good contacts
among German publishers, and felt frustrated when it was impossible for him to put these contacts at the disposal of his
friends; it is more than probable that Brod opened Franz Wer-
fel's way to glory, and he certainly eased Kafka's way into print.
By 1909 Brod was well known in Prague and Berlin as an enterprising young writer of considerable aesthetic finesse and an ad-
dict of Schopenhauer. Already he had written a collection of
novellas and a volume of poetry (published in 1907), and his
1908 novel, *Schloss Nornepygge* (Castle Nornepygge), had created
a remarkable stir among the Berlin expressionists. The following
year his novella *Ein tschechisches Dienstmädchen* (A Czech Servant
Girl) challenged both Prague Zionists as well as Czech patriots,
who argued in unison that the ancient Prague conflicts of na-
tionalities could not be solved as easily as the novelist thought.
Kafka, in some contrast to his friend Max Brod, had composed,
before going to Riva, only a curious medley of a few meditative
texts, a partly disheveled review of Franz Blei's rococo keepsake
for society ladies, not exactly Kafka's cup of tea, two fragments
of an early prose piece, and an important legal article on the in-

surance responsibilities of construction companies (published in 1908). Brod believed that Kafka was right in wanting to go to the air show. A new experience might break his writer's block, and he suggested that they might enter into a friendly competition: they would both write articles about the fashionable show of the new flying machines, and Brod would take care to see that Kafka's text would be published by a Prague newspaper.

IMMEDIATELY AFTER they arrived at Brescia, our friends were surrounded by a noisy crowd and found a rickety carriage that could hardly move on its wheels but whose coachman was in a good mood and rushed them, through nearly empty streets, to the Komitepalast (actually, the Palazzo Bettoni, via Umberto 1), where they were given the address of an inn that, at first sight, was the "dirtiest" they had ever seen. Kafka hated dirt viscerally, but he noted that the gesticulating innkeeper, "proud in himself, humble to us," constantly moved his elbows, "every finger a compliment." He ultimately resigned himself to ambivalent feelings of rage, dismay, and irony: "Who, one could ask, would have had the courage not to feel sorry in his heart for such dirt?" In a lighter moment, which Kafka remembered six years later in his diaries, on 4 November 1915, he walked on the Brescia cobblestones distributing a few *soldi* to the street kids (still in daylight), but as soon as the friends hired another horse-cab, they ran into trouble and the evening was nearly ruined. Kafka did not say where he and his friends wanted to go, but to judge from their habits, it possibly was a *café chantant*, if not a more disreputable place. The driver asked for three lire, the friends offered two, but the driver did not want to go, dramatically describing the terrible distance he would have to cover. The friends agreed to pay three lire, and after one or two turns, they arrived. Otto promptly refused to pay three lire for a one-minute trip, argued loudly with the driver, and wanted to call the police unless he was shown "the tariff." The driver produced a smudged piece of paper with illegible numbers. The tourists had been had; Otto, still screaming, made an offer of one and a half lire (accepted), the driver galloped with his cab off into the next narrow street, where, however, he could not turn around, and Kafka realized the coachman was not only enraged but melancholy as well. The friends had not behaved appropriately, and Kafka remarked ruefully, "You cannot behave like this in Italy. Perhaps somewhere it may have been right, but not in Italy." Yet again, he added cheerfully, you cannot become an Italian so quickly, within the short week of an air show.

Our friends spent a dreadful night at the dirty inn—"the robbers' cave," as they called it—and Max discovered, or later was thought to have discovered, a circular hole in the floor through which one could see the bar downstairs. Being an opera fan, he imagined that the evil Sparafucile, the killer from *Rigoletto*, might enter momentarily. But in the early-morning sun, the "bad hours of the night" were forgotten quickly, and the friends took the new tram, constructed for the occasion to transport people from Brescia to the plains of Montichiari, where the aerodrome, as it was called then, had been constructed. The traffic and the dust were frightful. Tram cars, bicycles, huge automobiles, horse-cabs, and donkey carts all moved on the narrow road (which continued on to Mantua). Despite the tram cars' being overcrowded, they casually stopped to take on even more passengers. At Montichiari, the masses streamed to an open field, guarded by decorative cavalry and border guards, and found the hangars, a platform, and other facilities including a post office.

The crowds did not see much flying in the morning. The winds blowing over the *brughiera* were too strong, and even when the committee functionaries substituted the white flag, suggesting the possibility of flights, for the green (which meant no flying), they did not assuage the anger of the public, which began to whistle in protest and tried to storm the restaurant. Many of the famous pilots did not go into action because their flying machines did not easily start. It was not a happy day for the Italians. Lieutenant Mario Calderara, darling of the patriots, could not crank up because his machine was out of commission temporarily, and so the French and Americans dominated. In the late afternoon, Blériot circled the airfield, ascending and descending again almost playfully but *hors concours*. The dour American Glenn Curtiss performed well, flying one and a half kilometers at an altitude of forty-five meters.

Kafka, trained as an insurance writer, had a sharp eye for technical detail, while his friend Max did not show himself too impressed by the feats of the flying machines and was more interested in the organizational and financial aspects of the meeting. Both Kafka and Brod basically wanted to write salable articles for immediate publication, and devoted a good deal of

attention to the social elite attending the events and the illustrious Italian artists in the audience or, rather, seen near the
hangars and in the restaurant. As self-appointed reporters, they
must, considering their changing takes and their almost incredible close-ups, have been moving quite a bit from one part of the
aerodrome to the other. Our Prague visitors both remarked on
the elaborate hats hiding the faces of the ladies and the curious
shape of their low-slung bodices, which made it imperative that
they constantly walk rather than sit. They must be embraced
tiefer, from below, Kafka wrote.

Brod and Kafka also both noticed the presence of Giacomo
Puccini, admired much more by Brod than by Kafka, who did
not care about opera and simply said that Puccini had the nose
of an alcoholic. Gabriele d'Annunzio, king of the air show—be-
having like a true showman, giving interviews to the press,
reciting a poem about Icarus—presented a fragile figure in his
white suit, always moving to strike a photogenic pose with a famous pilot or a principessa. He was certainly a man to be
watched, and for many reasons.

"Early evening on the Italian fields" descended quickly, as
Kafka noted, but the pilots went on for a while. Glenn Curtiss,
tired and grave, was applauded, and Henri Rougier, another
crowd-pleaser, ascended quickly in his "heavy plane," outdoing
Blériot—although by now it was nearly seven o'clock, after
which the flight results would not be registered officially. The
waiting cabs, carriages, and trams did not budge, for everybody
admired Rougier and waited for more. Our friends, who had a
long way to go, fortunately found a rattling jalopy (without a

driver's seat), and the jolly coachman took them to the Brescia station, where (after the experience of the preceding night) they took the train back to Desenzano, hoping it would be easier to find lodgings there. They did not fare better than in Brescia, and possibly worse; there were hundreds of pictures of saints in their room, Max remembered hyperbolically, and from under these pictures bedbugs appeared and attacked en masse. Although the Prague tourists may have had a high level of tolerance, considering Bohemian hotels and inns, they quickly moved out of their room and spent the night on a park bench on the Desenzano quay, awaiting the morning steamer, which safely returned them to Riva.

In their enthusiasm, the friends may have overlooked the repeated newspaper appeals of the air show's organizing committee to the citizens of Brescia to make apartments and rooms available to visitors and tourists. The committee urged the Brescians to live up to the town's grand reputation as a most hospitable place and, with the usual rhetorical flourishes, called on them to remember that it was a matter of Italian patriotism to help the committee as much as possible. Our friends, who were not concerned with international politics, may have underrated the Italian temper of the moment: Bosnia and Herzegovina had been annexed by the Habsburg monarchy the year before, and Italy (though formally allied with Germany and Austria) was making efforts to renew contacts with Britain and France and to come to an understanding with Russia in order to "consolidate" the situation in the Balkans—that is, to block further Austrian expansion there. Italian nationalism was flourishing, and the *irredenta*, belligerently deploring Austria's continuing power over the Alto Adige, Trieste, and Istria, was alive and well. Max Brod noted that people in Riva occasionally talked about tensions and about subterranean arsenals established in the mountains, but, he added blithely, nobody believed these things—war was an "irreal concept." True: Brescia was overrun by visitors to the air show and it was difficult to get rooms, but I cannot entirely free myself of the suspicion that our three innocents abroad overlooked the anti-Austrian mood of the people, especially in the border regions. Landlords were not particularly eager to serve *tre Austriaci* who (by the way) had little money in their pockets.

There is not much evidence of how the friends spent the rest of their meager vacation time. When they got back to Riva, it was nearly noon, Sunday, 12 September, and they were expected in Prague on the fifteenth. They probably lounged around the Madonna baths, Franz and Max scribbling away at their articles, concealing their ideas from each other, as Max remembered half joking, and asking Otto questions about details. Punctually, on 15 September, they were in Prague again to start working in their offices, and it is unknown how much they accomplished that day. That evening, Max Brod visited the editorial offices of the *Bohemia*, a daily of liberal and national orientation, and talked to Paul Wiegler, an eminent man of letters, and his assistant, Willy Handle, peddling Kafka's article. It appeared, with cuts made by Wiegler, on 29 September—possibly one of the first reports in German about the achievements of the new flying machines. Perhaps it is no exaggeration to say that Wiegler's own review article on d'Annunzio as "Pindar of the Airfield" ("Der Pindar des Flugfeldes," *Neue Rundschau* 21 [1910]: 1620–23), a shrewd assessment of his ambivalent character, owes a good deal to Kafka.

It is easy to forget that Kafka, at least before his last illness, traveled a good deal, with friends or alone—to Paris, Milan, and Zurich, not to speak of Vienna, Weimar, Budapest, and Berlin—and yet he rarely returned to spots he visited as a tourist. The notable exception was Riva, which he remembered in his life and in his art as a place of sunlight and sweet melancholy, free of anxieties. In the hapless sequence of later events that were to result in his two engagements to Felice Bauer (and their dissolution), Riva was, at the moment of crisis and desperation, a refuge from Felice and the place of an unforeseen and marvelous ten days' happiness with a very young Swiss woman. Kafka had met Felice, a successful Berlin business manager, at the Brods' in Prague, and began writing to her a month later (writing was loving). In a convoluted letter on 16 June 1913, he asked her whether she would be willing to entertain the question of marrying him—immediately trying to persuade her to reject his proposal by describing himself in the most unforgiving terms as "an ill, weak, unsocial, morose man, stiff and a nearly hopeless human being" (with a rather modest income of 4,588 crowns). As Elias Canetti has shown in his impassioned analysis of his letters, Kafka rhetorically turned against himself to avoid an engagement. In May and June 1913, he had at least twice invited Felice in his labored way to join him on a trip to Lake Garda, and now he was to go there all alone, without apologies.

Kafka's futile attempt to escape the Felice entanglements once more was well camouflaged as an inevitable trip to Vienna, where he was due to attend the Second International Conference for Rescue Services and Accident Prevention (9–13 September) in the company of his senior supervisors, Eugen Pfohl and Robert Marschner, whose speeches he had written; he also wanted to be present at one of the meetings of the Eleventh Zionist Congress (2–9 September); and then he planned a more private later excursion to Venice and Riva, where he wanted to spend a few peaceful days. Originally he had thought of going with Otto Pick, a Prague fellow writer and gifted translator of Czech, but the journey together from Prague to Vienna revealed that they were not ideal travel companions (Kafka thought that Pick tyrannized him, and vice versa), and while he spent some time with Pick in Vienna, he eventually left by himself for the Italian provinces.

On Sunday, 7 September 1913, the Prague visitors to Vienna took it easy. In the morning, Kafka and Pick collected their admission tickets to the Zionist Congress at the Residenzcafé, where they were joined by Lise Weltsch, organizer of the Prague Zionist Women's Club, and together the three proceeded to the Ottakring district to visit Albert Ehrenstein, an expressionist poet whom Kafka had met earlier in Berlin. Later they all had lunch at a vegetarian restaurant, the Thalisia, near the Burgtheater, clearly Kafka's culinary choice. In the early afternoon they went off to the Prater fairgrounds, together with thousands of other Viennese, bourgeois and plebeian, of many languages and ethnic origins. (I have been there recently, and the

Franz Kafka and his friends in the Viennese Prater, September 1913.

visitors have not changed much.) The friends stopped at various shooting galleries, bought tickets for a ride on a "Day in the Jungle" merry-go-round, and a famous photograph was made showing all four of them in a mock papier-mâché aeroplane against a painted backdrop displaying the Riesenrad (which appears in a famous scene in the 1949 film *The Third Man*) and two church steeples suggesting the city "below." There they are, the gentlemen all in spiffy attire and the young woman with a fashionable hat and elaborate *fichu*. (From left to right: Kafka; the poet Ehrenstein who wrote a few aviation poems among others, and died in his New York exile in 1950; Otto Pick, who was to die in London in 1940; and Lise Weltsch, who later married the Zionist writer Siegfried Katznelson and went with him to Israel.) I like to believe that it was Kafka who, remembering Brescia, suggested to his friends to climb into, or rather stand up in, the contraption to have the photograph made—which may explain his rare smile, the rather sullen faces of the other men (why should we have to do this, anyway?), and the quiet patience of Lise, who sometimes tended to irritate Kafka, but only mildly so.

The next day, Monday, 8 September, Kafka and Lise attended a session of the Zionist Congress (though she was not among the officially listed delegates), but it would be difficult to say that they did so with serious zeal or enthusiasm, at least from Kafka's point of view. He certainly did not listen carefully to the technical and financial discussion about funding new farms and settlements, and he noted in his diary that at the congress people "with small and round heads, and with firm cheeks, prevailed. . . . There were speeches in German without results, much Hebrew. The main work is done in small meetings. Lise let herself be dragged by all of it, without paying much attention [*ohne dabei zu sein*], throws little paper balls into the auditorium, cheerless [*trostlos*]." Kafka's "*trostlos*," disconsolate, placed at the end of a complicated sentence, may refer to Lise's attitude or to the entire scene.

I believe that Kafka wanted to leave Vienna as quickly as possible; he sat on the stone balustrade in front of the Parliament building (where the insurance conference was held), sadly walked through the streets, pondered the impossibility of any togetherness with Felice, and on 14 September took the fast train south to Trieste and went from there by boat to Venice, where he had to recuperate from a grotesque bout of seasickness. After he had written another despairing letter to Felice, he finally moved on to Verona and Lake Garda.

On 21 September, Kafka was in Desenzano again, ready to transfer, as he had done with his friends four years earlier, from the train to the lake steamer. He was sitting in the grass, watching the waves in the reeds, Sirmione to the right, Manerba to the left, and thought he was really happy because nobody knew exactly where he was. "In all the corners of my being, I am empty and without any meaning," he scribbled on a piece of paper that he transcribed for Felice only many months later, and told himself that he felt like a big stone inside, his soul being just a dim light. The day before, he had wept in a Verona cinema; that only showed that he was capable of enjoying human relationships vicariously but not of living them through. Yet change was imminent. As soon as he checked into Dr. Hartung von Hartungen's sanitarium in Riva, the stone came to surprising life again. There was a flirtatious Russian lady across the corridor and an attractive young Swiss girl (actually, from Genoa) in the room above his own. Kafka wanted to write a few fairy tales for the girl to read between meals; he noted that she blushed easily, especially when the chief physician was close by, and he sympathized with her irritation and pain when she had to speak about her own life. He asked himself, quite frankly, how many pleasures he was forfeiting by favoring the young Swiss, "almost a child," over the Russian lady, who might have invited him to her room for the night. Kafka and W. (or G.W.; he never revealed her name to anybody, as he had promised her) invented their own games; he knocked on the ceiling or listened to her coughing or her singing before she fell asleep. Sometimes she answered with her own knocking from above, in a rather innocent Morse code, for they had not agreed on any. He leaned out of the window to greet her when she did the same, or sat on the windowsill, eager to catch a fluttering ribbon that she let fly from above. All this happened without many words or labored letters—pure bliss, "the sweetness of melancholy and love." They went rowing on the lake. W. smiled at him in the boat—"That was the most beautiful thing"—and he felt like a romantic poet of old on a voyage to Italy when love was "only the desire to die and yet to hold on."

Unhappy Felice! She knew that something was going on but did not know what, and sent her friend Grete Bloch to Prague to discuss matters with Franz, who promptly fell in love with Grete, too. The affair with Felice dragged on for more than three years (the correspondence with Grete Bloch continuing as well), rich in misery and rare in consolations—until Felice visited Franz after his tubercular hemorrhage, in a little Czech village where he lived with his sister, after which the exchange of letters ceased, forever.

Kafka does not usually insist on the autobiographical meaning of his stories, but in the many fragments of the story *Der*

Jäger Gracchus, composed in 1916–17, he signals that his texts and his life hung together more closely than abstract criticism wants to permit. It is the story of a man who seeks quiet happiness, serenity, and salvation, and in the figure of Gracchus, the restless hunter, images of Wagner's "Flying Dutchman" and Ahasver, the eternal Jewish wanderer, are curiously combined. A barge that seems to glide above water brings Gracchus, who cannot die and yet cannot live either, to a little port town, and he is carried on a stretcher from the barge, across the town square to the town hall, where the mayor, named Salvatore (the one who can offer salvation), wants to attend to his needs. He listens to the stranger's extraordinary story: Gracchus died hundreds of years ago, but by a strange mistake the barge that was to deliver him to the netherworld inexplicably veered from the course and continues to carry him across the waters of the world. The mayor asks Gracchus whether he wants to stay in his little town, but Gracchus ironically tells him that he does not intend to do so, and yet, he adds, "I am here, more I do not know, more I cannot do."

It would be difficult to ignore that Gracchus plays on Kafka's name (the Latin *graculus* = the Italian *Gracchio* = the German *Dohle* = the Czech *Kavka*), as the German scholar Wilhelm Emrich long ago noted; that the mayor unhesitantly identifies his town as Riva; and that, as Hartmut Binder has shown, the topographical detail, exceedingly rare in Kafka's prose, fully corresponds to the town of Riva in Kafka's time—steps, a town square, a monument (actually, Prague's Saint Nepomuk, to whom Kafka gives a theatrical sword), an old church tower, a wall of rocks (once again the Rocchetta), and the Palazzo Municipio. The story, if that is what it is, reveals something about Kafka's restlessness when he went to Riva for the second time, as if on Charon's barge gone astray. Unable to love Felice and yet incapable of totally freeing himself of her, he sought, on the rebound, a glorious moment of blissful respite. "So you are dead and yet alive?" asks the mayor in the story, and the response can be found in Kafka's diary of the moments after he had met G[ertrud] W[asner]—in his wish to die and yet his desire to hold on to life, as if it were his last moment.

CHAPTER TWO

Interludes

THE INTERNATIONAL CAR RACES AT BRESCIA

The city of Brescia—third in population in the north of Italy after Milan, rich in commerce and industry, and Piedmontese Turin, with its Fiat factories and a pioneering film industry—had its own lively sense of civic pride and spontaneity, and in the first decade of the twentieth century it arranged competitions of the new industrially produced vehicles of modern speed—the bicycle, the automobile, and the heavier-than-air flying machine. The example being followed was France's, where bicycle and car races had already become popular events attracting thousands of spectators eager to see demonstrations of recent technology and daring courage. On 22 June 1894, twenty-one cars, variously powered by electricity, steam, and gasoline, had participated in the Paris-Rouen race. Soon the distances stretched from Paris to Bordeaux and return, and from Paris to Marseilles and back in 1896, by which year only two of forty-two cars were left to rely on the power of steam. The idea caught on in England and Germany, and in Brescia, where,

thanks to clubs like "Forza et Constanza" and "Audax," commitment to active sports was particularly keen; in 1904 the sporting
clubs there brought 2,300 cyclists to the city.

A group of prominent and well-to-do citizens in Brescia had
bought cars early, and their loosely organized circle of friends
and enthusiasts were the first to think of arranging automobile
competitions. Of the dozen or so citizens who discussed the possibilities of races around the city, one was a baron and three
were counts. These car fans, called the *buontemponi* (fellows who
liked to have a good time), were easily recognizable by their red
berets and huge goggles and, to much public annoyance, by the
clouds of dust rising behind their noisy machines dashing
through the narrow streets. These blithe men were enthusiastic
and enterprising, and in September 1899 they organized a four-
day automobile festival, the first of its kind in Italy. It combined
an elegant car show and an exhibition of new automotive technology with a road race in a wide triangle from Brescia to Cre-
mona, Mantua, and return via Verona. It was repeated the
following year with great success.

Fortunately, the history of the Brescia car races has been
chronicled by Albino Micelli, and I can rely on his *Storia del circuito automobilistico di Brescia-Montichiari* for a chronicle of events
that enables me to determine in what way the car races antici-
pated the Brescia air show of 1909. In September 1900 an infor-
mal committee began its discussion of future automotive
events. Since a number of industrialists participating wanted to
compete with the Milan industries, a *settimana automobilistica
di Brescia* was discussed, a weeklong technological exhibition

combined with a road race along the Brescia-Cremona-Mantua-Brescia triangle. The only trouble was that the Milan Auto Club revealed its own plans for a 1905 industrial show, and the Brescia committee quickly responded by rescheduling its Automotive Week for early September 1904. On 10 September the cars roared off on the Montichiari road to compete on the big triangle, a stretch of 370 kilometers, and among the many prominent drivers still remembered today, Vincenzo Lancia (of Turin, in a Fiat) won in three hours, nine minutes, and fifty-six seconds (averaging a speed of 115.7 kilometers per hour), followed by the rich Sicilian entrepreneur Vincenzo Florio (with a Mercedes in his stable) who instituted the famous Florio Cup, carrying an award of fifty thousand lire. It was Florio who suggested that "free races" be held through the fields outside of Brescia, the *brughiera* (later the aerodrome's location), and among the most effective members of the organizing committee, the press repeatedly mentioned Conte Oldofredi and a youngish sports enthusiast, Arturo Mercanti. Four years later they ranked as the most outstanding members of the new committee promoting the air show at Brescia.

After the success of 1904, grand plans were in the making for the car races in 1905, but rather unexpectedly, planners ran into difficulties with the state authorities, in the shape first of the national railways and then of the ministry of war. It turned out that during the 1904 races, the drivers had used many railroad crossings by tacit agreement with the local stationmasters or the regional administration, but the national authorities declared that unauthorized arrangements could not be taken for granted indefinitely, and the committee was hard-pressed to come up with alternate routes skirting the railroad system. The committee considered, at various times, a route going into the mountains north of Brescia leading to Gardone or Desenzano, on Lake Garda, so well known to Kafka, and the planners ultimately agreed on a shortened route of Brescia/Montichiari/Castiglione/Lonato and return, sixty-one kilometers in all, and scheduled the next race for September 1906. Unfortunately it was not to be, because the question of who would be responsible for order and security along the route, especially in sparsely settled places, was not easily answered. The committee asked the ministry of war to assign regular troops stationed in the region to do the job, but the minister flatly refused, saying that whatever the past agreements had been, he could not demand that regular troops provide services unforeseen in the army regulations.

The citizens of Brescia believed that the minister was acting against the best interests of the city (the possible loss of revenue involved was 200,000 lire), and when, on the evening of 22 July 1906, the music corps of the 74th Infantry Regiment played its usual Saturday concert on the Corso Zanardelli, the crowd began to whistle and to demonstrate against the army. The carabinieri and the local police (protecting the hapless musicians) clashed with the citizens, possibly for the first time in the name of technological progress. The local and national press took notice of the protests, there were more demonstrations on 23 and 25 July, the ministry of war was accused anew of acting against the city, and finally, Giovanni Giolitti, chief of gov-

ernment, once again rejected the use of troops and politely
suggested that other solutions should be discussed by all concerned.

Committee planning for the 1907 races increasingly relied on
close administrative and financial cooperation with the Milan
Auto Club, which, for the time being at least, supported the
Brescia projects. Even the question of security along the routes
was civilly resolved by the collaboration of the various cities. A
private force of nearly five hundred forest guards, local volunteers, members of fire brigades, and night watchmen was put
into service, and the local carabinieri joined ranks with them. A
good deal of money was spent to redevelop the sixty-one-
kilometer route; part of the road was tarred to reduce the chok-
ing dust, an underpass on the outskirts of Brescia had to be
built (to avoid the Verona railroad crossing), and an old fountain
at Castiglione regrettably had to go. The races were expected to
be international, and the rules were modified to please the
French. Some of the cars participating in the Florio Cup races
were admitted according to the content of their cylinders, others according to actual gasoline consumption. Italian (mostly),
French, and German drivers competed on 1 and 2 September
1907, and the Italian Fernando Minoia won the Florio Cup,
while the Italian Umberto Cagno achieved an average speed of
116 kph. (Cagno was not able to repeat his success when two
years later he switched to an airplane and competed in the Brescia air show.)

It is quite possible that lack of support for the car races
forced the Brescians to create an air show. Soon Milan ended its

cooperation, Bologna began to organize its own automobile races, and Brescia, sensing fierce competition on the roads, ingeniously lifted the races to the skies. Car races were briefly reinstated in 1921 (through the enthusiasm of Arturo Mercanti), when the crowds had a chance to watch the ill fortune of the famous Enzo Ferrari in a Lancia car and admire Maria Antonia Avanzo, the first Italian woman race driver.

FROM ICARUS TO BRESCIA: D'ANNUNZIO'S HISTORY OF AVIATION

In a surprising turn in his novel *Forse che sì, forse che no*, which d'Annunzio started to write in August 1909, the impassioned narrator, after telling us how brother and sister, both troubled emotionally, fall into each other's arms in an old castle, rather suddenly launches into a kind of aviation history from the mythical days of Icarus to the more recent actions of the "Latini" (Italians) who have inherited his ardor. In a wonderful intertextual two-page *abbreviatura*, d'Annunzio manages to quote himself as the "poet of the tribe," paraphrase Ovid, allude to Dante, compare Leonardo da Vinci to Daedalus, cryptically quote Nietzsche, and turn our attention to recent technological progress in Germany and the United States—totally ignoring the French, who were considered the leading force in aviation at the time, and were basking in the glory of Louis Blériot (mentioned by d'Annunzio only later), who had just flown across the English Channel to the astonishment of the world. While Marinetti and his Futurist friends poetically explore the fast motion of electrons and atoms and believe in the transforming power of future technology affecting society and language, d'Annunzio, while sharing their enthusiasm for the new machines, tends to look back to the mythical past, projecting ancient forms and figures into current advances. In his imagination, technological verve again and again clashes with the literary repertory of the educated humanist who puts himself at the service of the Italian nation.

The myth of Icarus offers d'Annunzio a splendid chance to bind together his ideas about flying, transgression, audacity, triumph, and death with an elemental scene of air, sun, earth, and sea (and to anticipate the noble fate of his fictional Giulio Cambiaso, the exemplary pilot who dares and dies). He quotes his artful sonnet *L'ala sul mare* (The Wing on the Sea), from his collection *Alcyone* (1903), and stylizes himself as the first visionary who has made his Italian compatriots aware of the possibilities of flying by retelling the age-old story of Daedalus's son (Ovid, *Metamorphoses* VIII). D'Annunzio has us watch the tragic moment when the waxen bond of Icarus's wings melts away in the heat of the sun, and the feathers, unlinked, scatter and tremble at every sigh of the air (lines 9–11 of d'Annunzio's sonnet literally reappear in the text of the novel), and the poet insists that it is the task of his fellow Italians boldly to continue what Icarus began. His play on Ovid (who himself quoted from the Icarus story in his *Ars Amatoria*) and an allusion he makes to Dante's *Inferno* mobilize the most august representatives of tradition to challenge present readers. "Who will gather" the scattered pinions, the poet asks, "who will bind them together" in a new way, far from the middle path (*dal limite medio*), and undertake a "mad flight" (*il folle volo*, *Inferno* XXVI, l. 125)? Dante ascribed this mission to Ulysses, who went beyond the known frontiers of the world and, unlike his Homeric predecessor, never returned home, dying, like Icarus, in the maelstrom of the sea. Past, present, and future are one in a moment of decision; and d'Annunzio's rich and oscillating vocabulary suggests the strange contemporaneity of the "gallant hero" (*il prode*), as if from the knightly world, and the "pale wreckage" (*pallido rottame*), potentially bringing to mind the debris of a modern plane crash.

For d'Annunzio, it is Leonardo da Vinci, the "new Daedalus" and the "new Prometheus without chains," who transmits the Icarian ardor to a later world. Dramatizing a good deal, d'Annunzio sees "new human wings" on the plains, hills, and lakes of Italy, "reddened by the blood of courage, smashed like the bones of the bold, torn like their bodies, inert in death." Clearly, he is not describing historical events of nascent Italian aviation here (the first fatalities were German, American, and, above all, French) but preparing his narrative ground for the glorious death of his fictional pilot Giulio Cambiaso, reenacting the tragedy of Icarus, and exhorting us to appreciate the aviation records of Cambiaso's friend Paolo Tarsis, the novel's protagonist. D'Annunzio's admiration for Leonardo cannot come as a surprise, yet it is interesting to read, in Niva Lorenzini's instructive essay on d'Annunzio's source materials (1990), that Leonardo's aviatorial visions and drawings were closely scrutinized in a series of lectures given in Florence in 1909 and published by d'Annunzio's friend Treves a year later; they were attentively studied by the poet, as his copy in his private library attests. It is perhaps even more important to know that the last lecture, "L'aeroplani di Leonardo," by Luca Beltrami, was reprinted in the *Official Guide of the Brescia Air Show*, where it appeared (pages 16–26) immediately following the patriotic introduction and preceding an article describing the improvised airfield between Brescia and Montichiari; and it was Beltrami who (like d'Annunzio) went straight from Leonardo to Otto Lilienthal, the undisputed pioneer of the new flying machines.

Writing about the German aviation pioneer Otto Lilienthal (whose name he does not explicitly mention), d'Annunzio combines his favorite Icarian strain of images with his old admiration for Friedrich Nietzsche, whose idea of the heroic superman helped to shape his pilots Cambiaso and Tarsis. Lilienthal, "a barbarian of the north," struggled with the the shadows of Icarus in an almost rustic and idyllic way; he imparted, the poet suggests, "a lively curve" to "ribs of reed," covered the wings with a most gossamer web, and listened to the wind—yet not only to the wind but also to the words of his forerunner, *il precursore*, who said that man lacks the soul of a bird and should impart a bird's soul to his own spirituality. I am inclined to believe that the voice of the forerunner is that of Zarathustra, ever "ready to fly" (iv, 18), or of Nietzsche himself, who, as one of the "astronauts of the intellect," in the concluding exhortation of his "Dawn of Day" (*Morgenröte*, 575) sings out his praise for bold birds: "They rise far above our heads and our failures, and from their height try to look far into the distant horizon and see hundreds of birds much more powerful than they are, striving whither we ourselves have also striven, and where all is sea, sea, and nothing but the sea!"

The Icarian and Nietzschean perspective, basic to the novel, inevitably blinds d'Annunzio to Lilienthal's actual theroretical and technical circumspection and performance; he rightly alludes to the sequence of Lilienthal's many glider experiments, but does not care to tell us that Lilienthal was, above all, a man of theory who first wrote on the flight of birds (a treatise published in 1891) and then twelve more scientific articles in which he interpreted his practical experiences in the light of his theoretical assumptions. There was nothing naïve about his experiments, mostly conducted on the outskirts of Berlin, at Lichterfelde, where he had to build himself an artificial hill to have an elevated jump-off point, a far cry from the wooden trampoline that he first used in his garden. He started in a fifteen-foot glider with a speed of thirty-three miles an hour, then experimented with a biplane structure (credited by d'Annunzio only to the Wright brothers) and a little motor, and lastly went up one day in an old apparatus that disintegrated; he fell to a miserable death on 9 August 1886. D'Annunzio writes that "he implanted the shape of his dead body on the harsh Germanic earth" as Icarus once inscribed himself "on the waves of the Hellenic sea."

D'Annunzio's portraits of the brothers Wilbur and Orville Wright (he never mentions their names, either) insist on their lonely, taciturn, and distant charm, not on the precision of their experiments or on their remarkable inventiveness. He describes them as Lilienthal's disciples, which was true in a sense, though they also studied the American experiments of Samuel Langley and those of their French ally Octave Chanute; and he makes a good deal, perhaps rightly so, of their decision to remove themselves from other people—that is, to their camp at Kitty Hawk, a sandy peninsula along the North Carolina coast, where they nourished their hopes to vanquish "hollow heaven." He calls their first controlled flight of fifty-nine seconds, on 17 December 1903, a "miracle" happening on a "rough winter morning, on naked dunes shaping a bay open to the ocean."

D'Annunzio does not say that the "miracle" was achieved by systematic experimentation and endlessly repeated test flights, characteristic of the silent "Ohio brothers," but the readers of a novel are not to be burdened with the technological complexity of their innovations. He does write that they attached two propellers (driven by a twelve-horsepower motor) to their glider, but they also added a rudder and, most important, achieved controlled flight by "warping," that is, by twisting the trailing edges of the wings, a mechanical arrangement used in one form or another by all modern aircraft, as Robert Wohl has observed. Yet we easily forget that the Wright planes were still elaborately catapulted from a derrick and ran along tracks before rising in the air. D'Annunzio cannot resist his inclination again to mythologize (and, as far as the Wright brothers were concerned, in full consonance with the French media), and we are left without knowing anything about the sharp business acumen of the Wrights and their later change of roles.

The serious sons of a Protestant bishop (Wilbur went to Yale originally to study theology), the Wright brothers turned themselves into inventors in their little printing and bicycle shop and later at Kitty Hawk; Wilbur, with his polished shoes, stiff winged collar, black tie, and famous golf cap, demonstrated to astonished Europeans in early August 1908 what the Wright planes could do, and on 31 December he won the Michelin Prize for the world's endurance record, staying aloft for two hours, twenty minutes, and 23.5 seconds. Subsequently the brothers turned their attention to selling patents and inventions; they suspiciously guarded the details of the contracts, through agents and sub-agents, with the U.S. Army Signal Corps and with foreign governments, including those of France, England, and Germany. They acted like industrialists with almost global intentions.

D'Annunzio's ideological attitude of Italy First! emerges clearly from what he has to say about Icarus, Leonardo, and the northern barbarians, and, more strikingly, from what he does not say or chooses to ignore, that is, the predominance of French aviation in Europe, especially after the Wrights returned to the United States. (British military authorities hesitated to invest in the new flying machines, and the Germans were content with the progress of Graf Zeppelin, though that was to change in 1912.) In his brief paragraphs about early aviation, once he has given the Wrights their due, he immediately returns to the Latini, who, right away, commit themselves to redressing (*alla riscossa*) the balance of achievements and gather to show their skill, courage, and inventiveness. Never mind the French, with the exception of Blériot, who turns up in the novel later.

Here is a new Olympia of competing aviators; and if, just recently, "fast cars of steel and fire" had annihilated time and space, now the "Daedalian wings" triumph over time, space, and gravity, and heaven itself changes into an immense *Stadion* framed by clouds, mountains, and groves.

D'Annunzio does not write about French aviation, but at least in 1908–9, it far surpassed the Italians, who were still unable really to compete with France's industrialists (with the exception of Anzani), investors, and best pilots. He does not tell us about Captain Fernand Ferber's famous book about the future of aviation (published in 1909) or about Clément Ader's earlier experiments, and he does not mention the first European airplane factory, at Billancourt, managed by the brothers Voisin, who developed their experimental kite-prototypes, dragged along the Seine by motorboat, into fully fledged planes that no longer needed catapults or rails. Wilbur Wright had trained a small group of aviators in France, including Comte de Lambert and Paul Tissandier; other pilots learned their craft independently, built their own machines, or used those produced by the Voisin *frères*, adapting them to their own experiences. *Tout* Paris was enchanted by the rich young Brazilian Alberto Santos-Dumont, who had read too much Jules Verne back home on the coffee plantations and came to Paris to construct dirigible balloons and, later, planes in which he whirled around the Eiffel Tower. Aviators like Henri Farman, flying Voisin machines, and Hubert Latham, a gentleman famous for his smart suits, attracted tens of thousands to the army grounds transformed into an aerodrome at Issy-les-Moulineaux, near Paris, and demonstrated that the French were ready to challenge America. The grand air show at Rheims on 22–29 August 1909 amply fulfilled their great expectations.

THE RHEIMS AVIATION WEEK
(22–29 AUGUST 1909)

The years 1909–12 were years of national and international air shows, and the Grand Aviation Week at Rheims, or rather at the nearby Bétheny airfield, set a glorious example that was often imitated but rarely if ever equaled. The participating pilots were mostly French, including Blériot (not in his best form), Hubert Latham, Louis Paulhan, and Eugène Lefebvre, always ready "to waltz in the skies." There were Glenn Curtiss of the United States, George Cockburn from England, and Comte Ernest de Lambert, actually a subject of the Russian tsar. Unfortunately, Santos-Dumont, the rich Brazilian dandy, inventor, and darling of the Parisians, did not finish the construction of a new plane and decided not to participate. All hopes that the Wright brothers would come were dashed when their business sense prevailed and Orville, hoping to conclude a lucrative deal, went instead to Potsdam to show huge crowds there, and the German crown prince, what his plane could do. Ideas about the military use of planes were not yet primary (except in the minds of early science fiction authors), and the Wright brothers thought in commercial terms, ready to license their patents to the highest bidder under strictly guarded legal conditions.

In the organization of the Rheims week, a mighty confluence
of money and industrial power was clearly visible. French interests were represented by the the Marquis de Polignac, who also
happened to be the chief officer of the Pommery champagne corporation, which was heavily involved in building the new aerodrome and subsidizing the awards, and a group of investors
under the name of Compagnie Générale de l'Aviation. These financiers put up forty thousand francs, floated their stock at the
Paris Exchange, and, after all was done, made a clear profit of
more than twenty times their initial investment. Half a million
people were to pay for attendance during the week, and many
more watched events from the elevations surrounding the airfield. All in all, thirty-eight planes were formally entered in the
lists, but because a few were not ready, only thirty-four machines competed, of which thirteen were monoplanes and
twenty-one were biplanes. In addition, there were two dirigibles: the military and imposing *Colonel-Richard*, commanded by
Henri Kapfèrer, and the more pliant *Zodiac III* by Comte Henri
de La Vaulx (later one of the sensations at Brescia).

A good deal of money, prestige, and fame was at stake. The
American expatriate and flying enthusiast James Gordon Bennett had endowed an award of five thousand dollars to go with a
decorous cup to the fastest aviator; there was also the Grand
Prize of Champagne for the longest distance flown, thanks to
the Pommery corporation, which donated 200,000 francs in
prize monies, and an award for altitude, another one for circling
the aerodrome in the shortest possible time, and a prize for flying at least ten kilometers with one or two passengers. The diri-

gibles, too, were to compete for a stretch of fifty kilometers. (Most of these prize categories were duplicated by the organizers of the Brescia air week.)

Never before had an air show attracted so many important politicians, diplomats, and industrialists, though intellectuals, artists, and poets were notably absent. In spite of occasional torrential rains, the president of the republic and Mme Fallières and their entourage visited the hangars (when there was no flying), Mme Fallières talking to Mme Blériot about matters of mutual interest, while Hart O. Berg, the Wrights' business agent in France, explained to the president how Wright planes were catapulted into the air. From England came Lloyd George, chancellor of the exchequer, from Brussels Crown Prince Albert and Princess Elizabeth, and the American ambassador accompanied Mrs. Theodore Roosevelt and her children. Every time a record was broken, the gypsy orchestra at the restaurant played the "Marseillaise."

On the eve of the show, after the rain, the Marquis de Polignac cut a dashing figure, prancing across the soggy airfield (the pilots were more concerned about keeping their magnetos dry), and on the morning of the first day 100,000 people showed up, most of them having bought inexpensive tickets. The crowds began to push against the barriers, and General Valabranche ordered two groups of his mounted dragoons to gallop against the disorderly to keep them in line, as if they were Communards. Active women had their day when two hot-air balloons rose from a field nearby, among the balloonists being Mme Blériot, but others were less happy. The aviator Henri Rougier (later to be one of the stars at Brescia) started his plane in the wrong direction and had to land perilously close to the spectators; a certain Mme Villars, suddenly seeing the plane braking in front of her, fainted in the best Victorian manner, and a less fortunate young woman who had just enjoyed her sandwich in the meadows was hurt on her ankle by Rougier's undercarriage, though the physician said it was not anything dangerous. (I shudder to think of the insurance problems if the event had taken place on an American airfield.) On the third day, Henri Fournier's plane crashed and, a little later, so did Louis Breguet's. On the sixth day, Paulhan, hoping to start for the distance competition, found his machine caught in a sudden gust of wind and pushed down against the runway; one wing broke, the propeller was destroyed, and Paulhan's last chances to compete for the award were gone (he was observed to weep). On the final day Blériot was lucky to escape alive from a burning plane. He had started early to ready his machine for the last race when the spectators noticed that his motor was aflame in midair. Blériot tried to land briskly, but the plane crashed. He himself emerged on fire and rolled on the soil to extinguish the flames; behind him the plane burned in a cloud of black smoke. Blériot was in shock, having suffered a wound on his forehead and a shoulder injury, and his hands were burned—no surprise that it was difficult for him to compete a week later at Brescia.

Drama was not lacking, but it also turned out that good and prolonged training and discipline were more effective than improvisation or braggadocio. On 28 August, Curtiss, whose calm was praised by all, won the coveted Gordon Bennett Cup for flying twenty kilometers in twenty-five minutes, forty-nine and one-fifth seconds. When all the other awards went to French aviators, at least one patriotic newspaper insisted that they had conquered the skies *pour la gloire et pour l'honneur de notre race* (though "race" did not yet mean what it came to mean thirty years later). Latham went up to 155 meters (within a year he was to reach one thousand), and Blériot, before crashing, did ten kilometers in the record time of seven minutes, forty-seven and four-fifths seconds. Farman was awarded the Grand Prize of Champagne, flying a distance of 180 kilometers in three hours, four minutes, fifty-six and two-fifths seconds, but his achievement was much debated by the press and by the spectators, who noted that his noble competitors Latham and Paulhan had had to fight strong winds, while he had flown when the air was calm. People wanted the glory of France defended, at least in this instance, in a more adventurous and less petit bourgeois way. He was the right man at the right moment, a reporter remarked, and though a few aviators protested the decision of the jury, the judges ultimately declared that he had fulfilled all rules and regulations.

CHAPTER THREE

The Organization of the Brescia *Circuito*

A S WE HAVE SEEN, it is more than probable that the Brescia air show—the first in Italy and, after Rheims, the second in Europe—was organized because international automobile races, the undisputed glory of the city so far, were also being planned for Milan and Bologna, and the citizens of Brescia wanted something to be proud of, without the competition of their neighbors. Historical reminiscences were not much in evidence or in the mind of the people; only later did Brescians come to remember the gifted physicist Francesco Lana Terzio, S.J., born in Brescia in 1631, who had written two dissertations about a flying boat, lifted above the water by four balloons, and, in modern times, Achille Bertelli, another son of Brescia, who in 1903 had experimented with his *aerocurvo*, a strange combination of balloon and airplane (it never functioned properly, and when a friendly army captain in Rome gave a demonstration, the contraption crashed and the captain gravely hurt his leg). There had been traveling shows by individual pilots (for instance, Léon Delagrange), but now it was time to organize an air show as popular as the car races. It may have been the untiring Arturo Mercanti, secretary general of the Italian Touring Club, who, perhaps with Conte Orazio Oldofredi, took the initiative. In 1907, Mercanti had been in France to observe the experimental flights at Issy-les-Moulineaux, and Wilbur Wright took him for a brief flight of two kilometers, only fifteen meters above ground, but with an average speed of sixty kilometers per hour. On 12 December 1908, the city council unanimously decided to allocate fifty thousand lire seed money to the air show, and technical preparations started in earnest. On 18 February 1909, a technical delegation inspected the location of the future airfield on the flatlands halfway between Brescia and Montichiari, and on 29 May, a high-ranking French delegation, including Blériot, his disciple Leblanc, and the president of the French Aero Club, Ernest Archdeacon, came to Brescia and met the Italian promoters; Blériot assured the Italians that he would certainly participate. The future air show was discussed in the local press, and it seemed opportune that the show coincided with the unveiling on a national holiday of a monument to Giuseppe Zanardelli, famous city son and former chief of government, to be attended by H.M. the King, together with many of his ministers.

For the organizing committee—or rather its two branches, an honorary and a general committee—an elite of officers, civil servants, politicians, industrialists, sports functionaries, and a few notables from abroad assembled. The prefects of Brescia and Milan were listed on the august seventeen-member honorary committee, together with the army commanders of the Brescia region, the presidents of the competing Italian Aeronautics and Aviation Societies, and the director general of the Italian Automobile Touring Club, as well as the publisher of Milan's famous newspaper *Corriere della Sera*. There was also the Comte de La Vaulx, founding father of the Fédération Aéronautique Internationale, who was to arrive in his dirigible *Zodiac III*, and Cortlandt Field Bishop, president of the American Aero Club, who attended the events faithfully. Among the thirty-four members of the general committee, aristocrats, investors, industrialists, and engineers were highly visible, among them Gerolamo Orefici, Brescia's popular mayor; Conte Orazio Oldofredi, scion of Brescia's oldest feudal family going back to the thirteenth century; and the engineer Evaristo Stefini, who was to plan and build the aerodrome. These committees were, of course, far too unwieldy to organize matters efficiently, and they delegated their powers to an executive and a sports committee (of ten and eleven members, respectively) and two groups of *commissari sportivi*, one each for airplanes and dirigibles to verify technical conditions and to supervise the competitions. *Cavaliere* Mercanti and Conte Oldofredi were impossible to avoid, and Orefici long concerned with the well-being of his city, was everywhere.

Gerolamo Orefici (1867–1932), son of a Brescia lawyer and a lawyer himself, was a longtime active liberal democrat of strong anticlerical leanings, and he made his swift political career from town councillor to two terms as mayor (1906–12) as a member of the local Zanardelli organization. He liked to insist on his artistic and especially his musical interests, yet he was also inde-

Caricatures of four prominent members of the air show's organizing committee—
Oldofredi, Mercanti, Stefini, and Orefici—published in the Guida ufficiale
to the air show.

fatigable in modernizing the city and unifying all its services
(trams, electricity, and such) in a single municipal enterprise,
welcomed by the citizens in popular referenda without much

opposition. He was strongly committed, both as mayor and, later, as vice-president of the Association of Italian Communes (where he loyally collaborated with its president, the Catholic antifascist Don Sturzo), to push for wider educational and medical support for the underprivileged, founded schools for children with learning difficulties, and organized a dispensary to help tubercular patients. Orefici was not *sportif* himself but actively championed the Brescia car races and made certain that the city approved the air show, long before the Aviation Week was held at Rheims. In the restless year of 1919, he was not elected deputy for the Democratic Concentration, and it is possible that this defeat prompted him to appear, on 2 March 1924, at a meeting of the National Block to back Mussolini. He was elected to Parliament for the right and concerned himself with administrative and financial questions.

Conte Orazio Oldofredi (1875–1931) liked to organize sports events of many kinds, and during his lifetime was president or board member of at least a dozen commissions in various fields of athletics, including skiing and canoeing on Lake Garda, car racing, and flying. In the aristocratic tradition, he started out as a marksman, receiving international awards in Switzerland and Germany. He also arranged bicycle Grand Tours, and by 1899 had switched his attention to motorboat and car racing. He was the chief organizer of the Brescia automobile races of 1904 and 1907, and in 1908 went to Paris to learn more about flying at the First Paris Aviation Salon; being prominent among the Brescia committee members, he was appointed *commissario sportivo* for airplanes and dirigibles. He was a city patriot, but not exclusively so; in the year following the Brescia air show, he presided over an international bicycle race arranged by a provincial newspaper, and was among the promoters of the Verona and the Milan air shows, competing with, if not counteracting, the aviation aspirations of his Brescia fellow citizens. He was particularly interested in that Italian specialty, the group flight in closed formation; he organized a Paris-Rome-Turin flight and another one from Geneva to Tripoli and Benghazi and return; and while he certainly was among the early champions of the group flight, I cannot find any evidence that he was involved in d'Annunzio's or Mussolini's mobilization of that tradition for belligerent or fascist propaganda purposes.

Arturo Mercanti, born in Milan in 1875, was a man of hectic commitments and almost feverish exertions; a detached observer justly speaks about his "frenetic activities" in times of peace and war. Mercanti studied accounting and was among the early members of the Audax biking club, which quickly developed into an all-around gymnasts' association in the German *Turnverein* tradition; as an Audax member, he walked with others from Brescia to Mantua to test his mettle (203 kilometers), and after he had left behind two exhausted friends, he went on a bike tour from Brescia to Basel, Ostend, Dunkirk, Paris, Genoa, and back. By 1899 he, too, had shifted his attention from the bike to the automobile, anticipating the possible military use of vehicles of speed, and organized a volunteer corps of bikers and car drivers to defend, with the army, the western shore of Lake Garda against the "Reds" attacking from Verona. In 1906 he was secretary general of the Italian Touring Club, planning the

Brescia car races together with Conte Oldofredi, and he went to France in 1907 to observe the new aviation experiments.

It speaks for Mercanti's qualifications that the French appointed him referee at the Rheims competitions. Returning to the Brescia show on the first special train, he was active on four committees and as *commissario sportivo*. He founded, again with Conte Oldofredi, the Società Italiana Aviatoria and had his share in the first group flights. He fought in the Italian-Turkish war in 1912 (in which, for the first time in history, warplanes strafed enemy trenches) and in World War I, as a *bersagliere* and, after 1917, as an officer in the air corps. He was demobilized as a high-ranking officer with many citations and decorations, and, returning home, joined the fascist *avantguardia*. By 1922, Mercanti numbered among the *squadristi* (fascist storm troopers), came to know Mussolini closely (he offered him his car), and after Mussolini's march on Rome, was appointed director general of Italian aviation (1923–24). Sixty years old, he had himself recommissioned to fight in Abyssinia, led a detachment of armored cars there, and joined General Graziani, commander in chief, in Addis Ababa. Mercanti died in combat, fighting a group of Abyssinian partisans who had attacked an Italian train. The Futurist poet F. T. Marinetti, who, in his late sixties, volunteered in World War II to join the Italian forces operating near Stalingrad, could not have created a stranger figure representative of an entire generation of fascists.

Early in 1909 the appropriate committees discussed the location of the airfield for the competitions, and it was not entirely surprising that parts of the flatlands east of Brescia but closer to the town of Montichiari were chosen. The Brescia car races had used the even roads cutting through them before, and the Palermitan industrialist Vincenzo Florio had early on suggested that cars be allowed "free" races right across the plain. The *brughiera*, or heath, as it was called locally (citizens of Brescia often spoke of it simply as *la campagna*), extended roughly along the Brescia-Mantua road (now No. 236), bordered on the north by the first promontories of the Alpine ranges, the little elevation of Castenedolo on the west, and Monte Baldo, San Martino, and Solferino, the famous battlefield of 1859, on the east and south. If the *brughiera* had not been there, it would have to have been invented for air competitions, a promotor remarked—an expanse of little vegetation that to the eye was almost a desert or "a calm and immobile sea," as a local reporter put it. The committees resolved, by February 1909, to use an oval-shaped slice of the heath extending from where the Brescia-Mantua and Calvisano roads intersected (today, the site of the trattoria Fascia d'Oro and a bus station) to the south, and keeping the old Calvisano road inside the projected airfield for access to the wooden constructions to be erected, and as a runway. From an aviation point of view, the *brughiera* was an excellent choice, and planners for the Italian Air Force, for the Germans, and for NATO later followed the Brescia committee in recommending it.

The committee solemnly declared that the air show was arranged with the city of Brescia in concurrence with the Italian Aviation Society. A catalog of rules and regulations governing the events was written under the guidance of the Italian Avia-

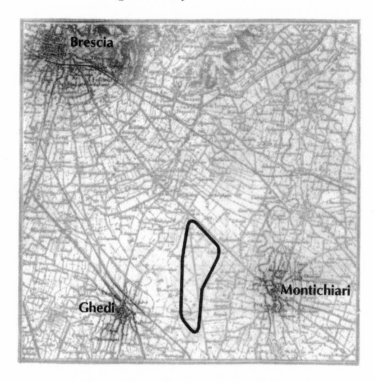

The location of the 1909 Brescia airport, from a contemporary map.

tion Commission and in agreement with the Commission Aeri-
enne Mixte de France (committee members had discussed all
finer points with the Marquis de Polignac, who had been in
charge at Rheims). The document was definitely not an amateur
performance, covering as it did the privileges and responsibili-

ties of aviators in a general section dealing with registrations (paragraphs 12–18); the technical control of flying machines, not to be modified during the competitions (19–23); the hangars (24–29), fully the legal responsibility of the aviators once they had placed their machines there; the difference between tryouts for individual competitions on certain days and obligatory qualifying flights on others—a compromise solution by which the sports committee hoped to satisfy the stricter concerns of the experts and the eagerness of the general public interested in bravura, show, and spectacle. It was hoped that the aviators would do their qualifying flights for individual competitions on 8, 9, 10, 11, 12, and 19 September, but, it was added, the results of these obligatory flights would have the same value as results achieved on any other day, preceding or following, in the tryouts. Rules and regulations were one thing, and the actual events another—the wind blew when and how it wanted, motors stalled, propellers split, planes crashed. The sports committee demonstrated unusual gifts of tolerance and improvisation. It was a particularly nice gesture of the committee to announce that twelve thousand lire would be divided among those aviators who competed but did not win a prize.

The official guide to the *Circuito*, published on 3 September, for the first time presented a complete list of aviators participating in the events, proudly noting that they were truly international. Actually, only one American was coming, and the competitions were mostly an Italian-French affair, as the Brescia car races had been. The guide registered the following entrants:

AVIATOR	MACHINE	MOTOR
1. Alessandro Anzani (*Italy*)	Avis biplane	Anzani
2. Louis Blériot (*France*)	Blériot monoplane	Anzani
3. Umberto Cagno (*Italy*)	Avis biplane	Itala
4. Mario Calderara (*Italy*)	Wright biplane	Rebus
5. Glenn Curtiss (*U.S.A.*)	Curtiss biplane	Curtiss
6. Mario Faccioli (*Italy*)	Faccioli triplane	Spa
8. Alfred Leblanc (*France*)	Blériot biplane	Anzani
9. Guido Moncher (*Italy*)	Moncher Elicoplane	Rebus
10. Henri Rougier (*France*)	Voisin biplane	Rebus
11. Leonino da Zara (*Italy*)	Miller monoplane	Miller
12. Comte Henri de La Vaulx (*France*)	Dirigible *Zodiac III*	—

People informed about recent technological advances and the Rheims races could see immediately that the gathering was a rather mixed bag of amateurs and professionals, illustrious stars and also-rans (reflecting the contemporary situation of aviation), and while the visit of the French dirigible was a welcome gesture to add to the attractions of the show, the committee would have been hard-pressed to say with whom the Comte de La Vaulx was going to compete. In practice, it turned out that the competitions were a matter of the professionals, among them Curtiss, Blériot (rather disappointing), Rougier, and Calderara; the others were far less visible, for they had to tinker endlessly with their contraptions, were unable to leave the ground, or immediately crashed, the pilots unhurt.

According to the program, the pilots of heavier-than-air flying machines were to compete for six major and three minor prizes (not all of them awarded, ultimately), and the chancellery of the Royal Court later announced that the king would give two more honorary awards, one to be received by a distinguished Italian pilot and the other for a successful airplane engineer. All in all, available prize money amounted to nearly one hundred thousand lire; local notables, among them Conte Oldofredi and *commendatore* Gino Modigliani, had substantially contributed from their own funds to make the awards attractive to Italian and international competitors. The major prizes and awards were announced as follows:

1. The Grand Prize of Brescia, for the aviator who flew fifty kilometers in the shortest possible time.

2. The International Modigliani Prize, for the aviator who reached the highest altitude.

3. The International Passenger Transport Prize, for the best time in flying one or two passengers for a distance of at least nine kilometers.

4. The Flying Start Prize, for the shortest time flying one kilometer, after a ground run of one hundred meters.

5. The Oldofredi Prize, for flying one kilometer in the shortest time.

6. The *Corriere della Sera* Prize, for the aviator who would fly twenty kilometers in the shortest possible time.

Chief Engineer Evaristo Stefini was appointed to plan the aerodrome and to construct the "wooden village" that was to be

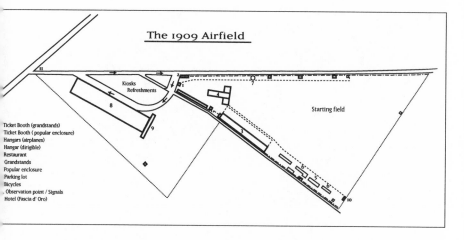

The Brescia airfield of 1909, in a simplified sketch, as published in the
Guida ufficiale *to the air show.*

its center. The basic architectural idea of the Brescia compound
was, like that at Rheims, the well-tested horse-racing arrangement; the new flying machines were competing in a kind of
Astor or Longchamps of the air. The concept of a grandstand
facing a racetrack was unchanged, though various technical facilities had to be modified or added. Ultimately, twelve wooden
hangars, all painted pink, were built, as well as a workshop for
the mechanics, a gasoline pump, a meteorological and anemo-
graphic station to register and record the force of the winds (donated by the ministry of agriculture), an observation tower for
the sports committee members, as well as a combination signal

An artist's view of the Brescia airfield of 1909,
also published in the Guida ufficiale.

mast and bulletin board imported from Rheims. The press
needed its own facilities: a special stand, a telephone, and a telegraph office with five tickers (two Hughes and three Morse) in
direct communication with Brescia, Mantua, Milan, and Verona.

The principal construction was of course the spacious grand-stand, the upper level for the elegant people (unavoidable in a society of marked class distinctions), the lower part for the pe-tit bourgeois, with a two-thousand-seat restaurant, a profitable franchise of the Bergamo Società dei Ristoranti Moderne. A new water main had to be laid, and there was ample parking space, in boxes or under a roof.

By the beginning of September, tickets to the air show went on sale at the committee offices on the Corso Zanardelli. They came in many kinds and price ranges, the most expensive being two hundred lire, which entitled holders to enter the airfield from 5 September to 20 September, the entire duration of the *Circuito*, and booklets of five transferable vouchers for a place on the grandstand (one hundred lire). People had to pay twenty-five lire for one-time tickets to the elevated level of the grand-stand and ten lire for a place on the lower level. Others could pay two lire for a day ticket to the general, rather plebeian en-closure, and it is safe to assume that Kafka and his friends bought these cheap tickets. Parking fees were five lire per day per car, twenty-five lire for the duration, and as it turned out, parking fees substantially contributed to the earnings. On the first day eight hundred cars arrived, and later 1,500 every day.

The sports committee worked out an elaborate system of sig-nals and numbers to inform the public what was going on. The marine code of communicating by flags and pennants, used by ships on the high seas, was adopted at the airfield; there was a highly visible flagpole and, in addition, a kind of bulletin board. A red pennant on top of the pole meant "flights to go on," white meant "flights probable," and green signified "no flights now." When Kafka and his friends visited their first morning, the green pennant had been hoisted, and the people, especially holders of two-lire tickets, vented their frustration in a concert of whistling and catcalls until the white and finally the red pennants went up. The right side of the big bulletin board showed "urgent signals," telling the observers who was flying (e.g., two white circles, one on top of the other, referred to Henri Rougier) or what the sports committee wanted (a black triangle, for instance, called for the help of mechanics). On the left side, "general signals" appeared (a white circle meant that a record had been broken) or a series of intricate numbers indicating the length of the flights, altitude, wind speed, and other circumstances ("102" meant one hundred meters of flight; "115" meant one kilometer; "125" meant one passenger on board; "186" meant the strength of the wind was three-fifths of a meter per second; "197" indicated the imminent arrival of the king). I assume that when the red pennant was up, most people preferred to watch the aviators than to bury their noses in the semiotic repertory that tightly filled the last pages of the guide.

Public relations were handled well, thanks to previous experiences with the car races, and the committees had no difficulties attracting press attention. At least sixty national and international newspapers and periodicals were represented at the show, and both the Stefani News Agency and the Associated Press sent the chiefs of their Rome offices. Of the important Italian newspapers, the *Corriere della Sera* (its influential publisher being a member of the honorary committee) delegated its star reporter,

Luigi Barzini, an inveterate traveler, and Ugo Ojetti, a critic of note. *La Stampa* (Turin) was represented by Gerolamo Bavione, *Il Resto del Carlino* (Bologna) by its editor-in-chief, and dozens of provincial newspapers competed with the more influential dailies. Editors of French aviation and automotive magazines came in full force, including Prince Troubetzkoy, who wrote for the *Locomotion Automobilistique*; reporters arrived from Warsaw and Buenos Aires; the *New York Herald-Tribune* and the *American Register* assigned people from their Paris offices to the Brescia job; and the *Vossische Zeitung* (Berlin) did not miss a chance to accredit seasoned members of its staff. Only Austrian newspapers showed no interest—Austria and Italy were still political allies on the international scene, but the tension between them was slowly rising.

THOSE WHO HAD chosen the *brughiera* as the most appropriate aviation field always assumed that wind and weather conditions were particularly stable, but during the night of 18 August, a sudden thunderstorm, possibly of hurricane force, nearly destroyed what had been built only weeks before. Shortly after midnight, the carabinieri of Castenedolo were notified that at 10:45 P.M. an abrupt gale, coming within fifteen minutes or less of heavy rains (lightning was seen in the distance over Lake Garda), had smashed seven hangars, sparing only that of Cobianchi and his plane; Lieutenant Calderara was far less fortunate. The commander of the carabinieri quickly informed the mayor of Brescia and the committee, and at almost the same time, the energetic owner of the Fascia d'Oro trattoria, at the junction of the Mantua and Calvisano roads, pedaled to Brescia on his bicycle and woke up Calderara in his hotel. Everybody gathered on the Corso Zanardelli—the mayor, Calderara, the prominent committee members, including Mercanti, Oldofredi, and Stefini, and the journalists from the *Corriere della Sera* and the *Gazetta dello Sport*. The question was how to get to the airport immediately to inspect the damage. Conte Oldofredi went home to fetch his chauffeur and car; other volunteers, among them a friendly dentist, readied their automobiles, and by 1:30 A.M. three cars rushed down the road to Mantua in the direction of Montichiari. People in the cars dimly perceived the crushed harvest on the fields, the devastated vineyards, and branches broken from trees, and when they came to the Fascia d'Oro they were stopped by a group of peasant women screaming that it was impossible to proceed because the road was blocked by fallen trees.

The airfield was desolate; a few disheveled workingmen who had slept in the hangars, three soldiers detailed to Calderara, and disoriented people from the neighborhood were all ready to tell their tales of woe: a peasant who had been riding his bike nearby, for example, had to abandon it and never found it again. Strangely enough, parts of the fence, together with a lonely ticket booth, were still standing in the void and one scaffold (to support the future grandstand) had resisted the force of the storm. The seven hangars were destroyed, the curtains over their entrances torn and scattered. On the ground, large sheets of mangled or irregularly buckled metal, the hangar roofs, could be found. Cobianchi's hangar had lost its roof; it was protected by the construction firm's temporary shack, which had been placed against it, and its curtains were tightly closed. Angelo Raccaglia, Cobianchi's mechanic, who had slept in the hangar, and Angelo Covadini, a guard of the construction shack, were among the heroes of the moment—suddenly awakened by the noise and fury of the storm, they had run out on the field half-blinded by sleep and rain, and tried to alert other workingmen and soldiers, but not much could be saved.

In the uncertain light of a few lanterns, Lieutenant Calderara talked to his soldiers and was, as the reporters noted, saddened "by the death of his machine." Yet, upon examining the damage, he quickly suggested that his plane had looked worse when he had crashed it at the Centocelle airfield near Rome (when training with Wilbur Wright), and he declared that the damage could be repaired before the official flights started. A soldier showed him that the propeller was untouched by the disaster (Calderara was to damage it later), and it turned out that the engine, too, was intact because it was still in its iron box; it was rescued by one Boris Werzov, a mysterious Russian lad who was living at Castenedolo at the time and had rushed through the storm to the airfield to offer his help. Calderara was fortunate in his misfortune; the press reported the news of the storm nationally and internationally, the Italian minister of war expressed his sympathy in a telegram, the army put its repair shops at his disposal (although he was a navy man), and Michel Clemenceau, son of the ex–prime minister of France, sent word that he was shipping his own Ariel, a Wright plane, from France to Brescia to be used in the coming events. Calderara went to work immediately; he telegraphed his friend and assistant Lieutenant Savoia to proceed to Brescia, assembled the usable parts of the machine, and trucked them to the city. His hands-on experience was useful when he later went to work in the American airplane industry.

When the sun rose above the destruction on the morning of 19 August, a squadron of *bersaglieri* arrived on bicycles to clear away the debris, and the soldiers were joined by one hundred workingmen under the supervision of city engineer Stefini, who began restoring the hangars immediately and continued with the construction of the grandstand and other buildings, as planned. The committees did not waste a minute; it was a matter of civic if not national pride (especially after Rheims) that the air show should go as scheduled. A committee proclamation predicted with a certain dash of optimism that with everybody's support, all the difficulties would be overcome, and they certainly were.

CHAPTER FOUR

The Events of the Air Show:
A Chronicle

B Y THE END OF AUGUST and early September, the Italian press provided the curious with reports about the wonderful events at Rheims, always stressing the primacy of Brescia for Italy; about the special trains carrying notables, aviators, and their flying machines from Rheims to Milan and from there to Brescia; and about the feverish preparations on the airfield only recently devastated by a thunderstorm. First to return, on a special train, were those important functionaries of the Brescia organizing committee (Mercanti *primus inter pares*) who had attended the famous *Semaine*. They were unstinting in their praise for the impeccable French organization, the excellent security measures, and elegant services, and they particularly noted the support given to the enterprise by the local champagne producers, in kind as well as in funds, the presence of the international press, and the *cinematografo internazionale*. The *commissari* traveled together with Alessandro Anzani, who had valiantly defended the Italian cause in the French air; when the prefect of Paris had praised Blériot's French achievements, Anzani told him politely but in no uncertain terms that Blériot had not crossed the Channel in a plane without an engine, and that his engine had been produced by the Anzani works, of Italy.

The press also listed the famous aviators who had boarded the special trains that also carried their machines: Blériot; Curtiss, who had officially represented the United States at Rheims; Henri Rougier and his machine; and the French dirigible *Zodiac III*, which was shipped in two freight cars. In the meantime, functionaries, workers, mechanics, and soldiers were busy preparing the airfield; the mayor, accompanied by popular committee members, shuttled back and forth between city hall and the airfield in an official automobile of the city of Brescia; in another car belonging to the provincial administration, the police chief of Brescia arrived. He decided to assemble fifty carabinieri at the Porro farmstead, near Montichiari, and another fifty at the Rodengo farm, near Castenedolo, to protect a security zone much demanded by the aviators who wanted to test their machines without obstructions.

On the morning of 3 September, at about ten-thirty, when Calderara and his mechanics were busy in their hangar and a group of committee members were supervising the construction of the telegraph office, a speeding car abruptly stopped at the main entrance to the field. Calderara immediately recognized the king of Italy, who was accompanied by one General Ugo Brusati and another officer. Calderara quickly approached the car, pilot's cap in hand, to welcome his supreme commander.

H.M. Vittorio Emmanuele III jumped "adroitly" from the car, the newspapers said, affably responded to the lieutenant's greetings, and immediately asked whether somebody would be willing to provide information about the *Circuito Aereo*. Protocol was preserved in spite of the surprise of the visit, *cavaliere* Mercanti (who else?) was close by, Calderara presented him to the king, and Mercanti took over to explain to His Majesty what had been built so far—the hangars, the committee offices, the control post, and the restaurant where the manager, Signor Guglielmo, offered refreshments and H.M. gracefully accepted a glass of San Pellegrino with ice (an inquisitive reporter discovered that the manager had stored 100,000 bottles of the water "to cope with coming events"). Calderara, Anzani, and Cobianchi rolled their machines from the hangars for inspection, but the king was especially interested in the American catapulting device that lifted planes of the Wright type into the air. He then expressed his gratitude to Calderara and the committee members and left with his entourage, taking the road to Mantua. He was to come again, more officially, when the new flying records and the award winners were celebrated.

Two aviators were now ready to test their machines, and the carabinieri had a difficult time clearing the field of cars and curious spectators, among them Prince Scipione Borghese and a few *elegantissime signore* who had assembled to have a look at the flying machines. The inventive industrialist Alessandro Anzani, attended by his engineers, was ready to test his Voisin machine with an engine from his own factory; he did not want to fly, but only to test the machine's balance, and it turned out that the position of the engine had to be corrected, possibly an overnight job. After the devastations of the August thunderstorm, Calderara was of course most eager to assess the performance of his reconditioned plane, and he did so two hours after the Anzani test, giving a signal to a soldier who activated the catapulting device at 4:30 P.M. The plane ran "as fast as lightning" along its tracks and ascended slowly to only ten or twelve meters, since Calderara did not want to waste gasoline. He described a near triangle of twelve kilometers, and stayed five minutes in the air. The result was that wires and ties had to be balanced anew. His second test was less successful; at six o'clock in the evening, with dusk slowly closing in, his machine shot "like an arrow" into the air, but almost immediately the motor began to sputter, and Calderara decided not to take any unnecessary risks.

The scene that afternoon was rather chaotic; the first tests were going on; the workmen were putting finishing touches on the wooden constructions; soldiers, mechanics, and the curious swarmed around the hangars; and the carabinieri tried to prevent the worst. The committee had good reason to close the gates and to issue a statement saying that only persons with valid tickets available at the committee offices and people attached to the various services would be admitted. For the first time the committee announced the dates of the flying competitions. Officially the *Circuito* would begin on 8 September (Wednesday), proceed through the twelfth (Sunday), and conclude with the final races and the presentation of awards on Sunday the nineteenth and Monday the twentieth. Aviators who were going on to participate in the Berlin air show later in Sep-

A hangar at Montichiari.

tember were excused from the last two days, but would have to forfeit the privilege of competing then. With a certain pride, the committee let it be known, too, that five hundred Americans who were eager to see Curtiss fly had arrived on the special train from Rheims (total travel time, seventeen hours). Among them were important American journalists, working for the *New York Herald-Tribune* and other newspapers.

On the following day the Italian aviators dominated the testing field, with rather mixed results. Anzani, the first to try, had to start three times before he managed to ascend and land without difficulty. He went up two meters in the early morning and flew a distance of eight hundred meters, checking on the stability of his biplane, but when he went up again later, something went wrong: he rose to not more than one meter, landed, and ascended again in spurts, "like a quail in a wheat field," a spectator remarked, hit against some deep furrows in the *brughiera*, twisted the chassis and the rudder's wiring, and had to be dragged to the hangar again. But he did not give up easily; at about 6:30 P.M. he went up for the third time, reached five meters, circled around the airfield, and landed easily enough while his team and the spectators shouted with joy.

Mechanical failures also marred the test flights of the untiring Calderara and the young aviator Mario Cobianchi from Bologna. In midmorning, when Calderara tried for the first time, his engine failed almost immediately, the machine touched the ground, and the impact twisted the rudder, a wire cut the propeller in half, and the lower part of the plane was slightly damaged. One of the soldiers attached to Calderara's team was the hero of the hour. His name was paradoxically Laruina, but he was an expert carpenter and promised to produce a new propeller over the weekend, which he did. Cobianchi, who had built his own plane with an engine of the Miller type produced in Turin, was even less fortunate; people heard his engine's mighty noise in his hangar and expected that he would start immediately, but "the power of the motor was too immense" and damaged the transmission box. The plane never left the hangar, and

Cobianchi began repair work right away, stoically as ever, people said.

The Monday papers reported that Sunday had been a quiet day, as it should be, except in the hangars of Anzani and Calderara, where engineers and assistants continued to work; Cobianchi's engine continued to cause trouble. On Monday and on Tuesday morning, the *brughiera* looked deserted, the reporters observed, but they noted that pilots and machines kept arriving—Glenn Curtiss, Umberto Cagno (Italy), Louis Blériot, and Guido Moncher, from the Trentino. Additional security details took over guarding the field, among them carabinieri on horseback and bicycles and even a squadron of the Milanese cavalry, the No. 7 Lancers. The complicated signaling system, little flags and all, was installed under the command of the Marchese Camillo di Soragna, a "brilliant naval officer." Both Curtiss and Blériot had been welcomed with full honors when they arrived at Brescia station; the mayor was on hand, and with him Conte Oldofredi and other notables, who went with the aviators to a reception at committee headquarters to meet Senator Federico Bettoni, president of the committee, and were later driven by the count to the airfield. Curtiss, usually very dour, was kind enough to say a few amiable words to reporters about the unusual beauty of the vast *brughiera* and the efficiency of the organization (which he did not know yet), and he also praised, almost demonstratively, the intelligence and expertise of his mechanics.

There was little flying on the afternoon of Tuesday the seventh, but the crowd grew by the hour, and the journalists once again remarked on the elegance of the spectators—"sports-mens" [*sic*], photographers, officers, functionaries, and ladies "lovely in their summer dresses with grand veils the vivacious colors of which were in distinct contrast with the gray and brown earth tone of the field." Expectations ran high that Curtiss would be flying: his biplane was taken out, but his mechanics only briefly tested the engine and immediately returned the plane to the hangar. That afternoon only Henri Rougier, the French aviator, went up in his Voisin biplane to twelve meters, circled the field, and returned with polished precision; and Anzani, ever ready to compete with the French, went up again to about ten meters, but by then it was almost night and the crowds did not even wait for the return of his flying machine to the hangar, leaving in their cars for Brescia. The real competition was to begin the next day at eight in the morning, and everybody wanted to be ready.

ON 8 SEPTEMBER, the first official day of the air show, nearly forty thousand people began to move on the roads to the airfield—on foot, on bicycles, in carts of many shapes and ages, in automobiles, and on a new Belgian-built steam tram that created more traffic problems than it solved. (The Brescia City Orchestra was to play a concert at the field, tried to get there, but gave up in the end.) Everybody and everything was shrouded in dust, and a reporter noted that there were two kinds of automobiles on the road: those that had been well kept in Brescia garages and carried ladies in impeccable veils, their faces untouched by the dust, and those overnight drivers who had to hide their elegance behind immense goggles and improvised ruffs of oilcloth, "ladies with faces a little gaunt, eyes marked by lack of sleep and made large and more expressive, as if under a voluptuous shadow." (The local reporter wrote in d'Annunzio's best manner.)

The title page of the Guida ufficiale, *published in September 1909.*

The show commenced rather inconspicuously; people were milling around rather aimlessly, planes were rolled out of the hangars and returned to them again, and five thousand hungry guests tried to storm the restaurant built for two thousand, now protected by a double line of guards, with waiters running through a protective echelon of *bersaglieri*. The wind was calm and the signal flag announced *si vola* (we fly), but spectators were restless and disappointed by the slow morning.

Obligatory flights were to begin at two o'clock, but the aviators, it seemed, were not in any particular hurry. Yet by three o'clock people had a hard time training their binoculars on individual flights, so much was going on concurrently. Anzani was trying, and Glenn Curtiss, the international hero and winner of the Gordon Bennett Cup, went up to an altitude of forty meters "like a gracious dragonfly," directly and firmly, and people had a chance to admire the splendor of his plane, the shining bamboo construction, nickel weldings, and wings of immaculate linen that "imbibed the wind," as it were; reporters compared his plane to the yacht of a rich sportsman. He flew a few delicate curves and turned his engine off before landing in grand style, greeted by sonorous applause, especially by the Americans in the crowd.

There was something melancholy about Blériot's first flight: he had just been informed that his friend Eugène Lefebvre had died in a flight accident on the field of Juvisy in France. (It was the second fatal accident in aviation history, the first one killing Lieutenant Thomas L. Selfridge of the U.S. Army in a crash with Orville Wright in Virginia on 17 September 1908.) Himself middle-aged, Blériot had not fully recovered from his recent accident at Rheims, and he took the pilot's seat with a bandaged arm and an aching leg. But he went up quickly, cruising lightly and like a bird above the *brughiera* before landing effortlessly, to much applause.

Calderara had just exchanged the original engine of his machine for one of the same type put at his disposal by Michel Clemenceau, and after the misfortunes of the preceding days he thought of a new method of ascending more quickly by taking off into the wind. He did not reach sufficient altitude, however: the plane took a sudden turn and went down fast, splintering the wood construction and lacerating the cloth wings as it crashed. Calderara himself escaped unhurt, emerged with his hands behind his back, his head low, and was immediately surrounded by people who wanted to help, as well as the *bersaglieri* and the cavalry. Nobody was certain that the plane could be repaired again.

Henri Rougier had commenced his flights early. When, at 11:45, his mechanics had rolled the Voisin biplane from the hangar, observers were astonished at how small and fragile it seemed, the cloth wings on a light undercarriage, like "a children's toy." Rougier ascended hesitatingly, but then the wings rose with the slight wind and his machine responded beautifully to his touch, describing a wide curve over the distant farms. Everybody was surprised that after he landed, the signals indicated that his had been a flight of not more than four kilometers. At 3:00 P.M. Rougier tried again—for the Grand Prize of the city of Brescia—but his engine stopped almost immediately and he had to land; the referees ruled that his attempt was invalid.

Alfred Leblanc, another French aviator, using a Blériot-type plane, was not lucky either. In ascent, many believed, he did not have Rougier's mastery; after landing and ascending again, he nearly completed a large circle around the field, but the engine stopped and he had to touch down quickly. It turned out that the propeller tip had broken off, and the plane had to be towed away for repairs. Later in the day, Leblanc tried again, but with indifferent results.

Anzani felt challenged by the French flights and, welcomed by the shouts and cries of the patriotic public, went up once more. He was immediately compared with that daredevil Lancia, the hero of the Brescia car races a few years before. But he did not succeed: his second attempt was not registered by the sports committee (it fell short of the one kilometer for the Oldofredi Prize), and the first had been too slow.

Eager spectators, who had arrived in the early morning, began to leave the airfield by midafternoon, and it turned out that the new tram could not carry the droves of passengers, who were storming the carriages and hanging from the platform. It did not have sufficient power, so the trains had to run in small sections, and the result was a traffic jam of unimaginable proportions. One unfortunate peasant fell off a carriage and had to be taken to the Castenedolo pharmacy, and it was rumored that he was hovering between life and death.

The second day of the *Circuito* began at an even slower pace than the first. In the early morning thousands of people (the ones with the least expensive tickets) arrived on foot, and the parking lots for more well-to-do spectators were not even half full by midmorning. It was warm, not yet hot, the sun hidden behind clouds, the air absolutely still. Perhaps the aviators were saddened, the press surmised, to hear that their French colleague Lefebvre, who was known to take risks, had died in a crash; only Anzani showed no signs of melancholy. There was silence in Cobianchi's hangar, Cagno tried to cope with his troublesome engine, and Moncher was mysteriously absent. People again began to show impatience, and *cavaliere* Mercanti, on behalf of the organizers, made a little improvised speech to calm the unruly masses. He told them that the aviators were allowed to choose their own time to start, and they did so carefully because the engines (except for the Wright ones) did not have any cooling mechanism and there was always a danger of overheating.

Once again the eager Anzani was the first to start, at 2:20 P.M., but he did not go very far, even when he tried for the second time. When Leblanc, who wanted to know how much runway he really needed for a "flying start," took up his "yellow butterfly," he made a sharp turn, and plunged into a little ditch, lightly damaging his plane; his second attempt that afternoon at least validated his competence, but not much more. Blériot was ready shortly after five o'clock, but he was not lucky at all; his motor suddenly slackened and he took a downward turn, touching the ground; he and his machine were unscathed, however, and he returned to his hangar under his own power. He went up again after six o'clock, but he had started too late, and his flight was not registered.

The stars of the day were Rougier, who in his first flight rose to twenty-five meters, and Curtiss, and the public vociferously acclaimed their skills. Rougier, in his second attempt, at 4:00 P.M., was again going for altitude: he ascended quickly in circles higher and higher, and reached what was believed by spectators to be an altitude of more than one hundred meters, though the sports committee confirmed that he had only reached ninety-three. After some discussion with members of the sports committee, and insisting that he needed a longer runway, not forty but at least sixty meters, Curtiss went for speed. He tried to achieve an undisturbed horizontal balance, nearly buzzed the enthusiastic grandstand, and after he landed, the referees confirmed that he had flown 1.5 kilometers in one minute and four seconds. Few people noted that while Curtiss was starting, Anzani, who had left his plane on the field, taxied his machine to the hangar, but it turned suddenly in an abrupt curve, and had to be dragged away by the mechanics. There was something wrong, and Anzani did not show up again.

The third day, 10 September, was the worst of the *Circuito*, and those experts who had been at Rheims must have remembered the heavy rains there that made flying impossible for nearly forty-eight hours. High expectations and unmitigated disappointments: the wind, under a leaden sky, was too strong; in the west, toward Ghedi, it was raining, and clouds and mists were drifting in from the north, over Lake Garda. "The *brughiera* was like a greenish sea that rolled toward the horizon," a reporter wrote poetically, "and the light dust storms there moved like the foam of rising waves." Holders of inexpensive tickets, always most eager to see the show and totally unimpressed by the poesy of nature, became impatient early on, when the green flag signaled that there would be no flights, owing to inclement weather. As the hours passed, people began to whistle as they had done previously, first sporadically and then in a well-concerted and noisy demonstration. Even *cavaliere* Mercanti did not dare to speak. The committee unwisely decided to hoist the white flag, promising against all meteorological evidence that there would perhaps be flying.

Reporters were busy nevertheless. Puccini, d'Annunzio, and Luigi Barzini had arrived, and the press corps had a good time running after the famous people. It was not hard to find Puccini, who did not budge from the restaurant and talked at length there about his new opera, *La Fanciulla del West*. It was less easy to keep track of d'Annunzio, who was busy visiting the hangars, striking poetic poses leaning gently on the planes (for the many owners of Kodaks), and trying to convince the pilots that while he was writing his Icarus poem, an intuition had told him "that one day he would be flying too." Luigi Barzini, who was as eager as d'Annunzio to fly, held court among his colleagues and his women readers, who admired his elegance, his sharp profile, and his exotic attitudes, which he had cultivated after many years abroad. Yet, in the absence of any flights, the poet won the day: "D'Annunzio's Day!" the local newspaper declared in a headline. The famous people had to stay overnight if they wanted to

watch action on the field, and so it happened that they were
watched, in turn, by Franz Kafka and his friends, who arrived
from Riva.

The fourth day, 11 September, brought calm air again, and
new waves of visitors from the cities of northern Italy and the
border regions. The morning was slow, with only Blériot trying
at eleven o'clock, but his machine refused to start; however, the
later afternoon was really exciting. The journalists, amazed by
the number of first-time visitors from Bergamo, Verona, Cre-
mona, Parma, and (Austrian) Bolzano, ascribed the renewed interest, after the disappointments of the previous days, to a
growing awareness that people had a chance to watch a chapter
in the long story of humanity triumphing over the forces of nature: "though great progress had been made, a solid and efficient
[flying] machine had yet to be constructed."

The roads were as terrible as on the first day, if not worse,
and the new tram, which showed a tendency to derail, was certainly a mixed blessing, as Kafka noted. People spent the time
talking and whistling in protest—an established tradition by
now—ate their sandwiches, and observed how the elite slowly
congregated; reporters enthusiastically acknowledged the presence of many financiers, captains of industry, artists, and writers, including Puccini and d'Annunzio. Kafka and Brod moved
around the *recinto*, but their presence was discovered only fifty
years later by Italian commentators. Influential publishers and
their star reporters, like Luigi Albertini and Barzini of the *Corriere della Sera*, were always seen together; and when all flights

were canceled for a while, plane watchers turned their attention to the noble ladies parading in front of the grandstand or up in the restaurant: Princess Letizia, wife of the Duke of Aosta, closest to the throne, Princess Borghese (née Countess Ilona Apponyi, from Budapest), and Countess Annina Morosini, lady-in-waiting to the queen. Kafka and Brod offered full accounts of their voluptuous fashions in their articles for Prague readers, and suggestive implications were not entirely absent from their reports.

At four o'clock the flying really commenced, and for two hours and more Blériot and Rougier started and landed (Blériot four times and Rougier two) to test their machines, at least once simultaneously. When Blériot flew with Leblanc at his side, people began to shout "D'Annunzio! D'Annunzio!" believing that it was he who sat with Blériot, but the poet was watching all the flights from the hangars. There had been rumors that Curtiss would start, and occasionally people shouted "Go, Curtiss! Go!" Shortly before 6:00 P.M., Curtiss, still intent on competing for the Grand Prize of Brescia, went up with his "gigantic skylark" and began to curve above the "fascinated, hushed, hypnotized" crowds. "He flies away from us," Kafka wrote, "flies over the plain that extends before him, to the forests in the distance that seem to emerge just now. For a long time he cruises over the forests, he disappears, we see the forest, not him. Behind buildings, from God knows where, he appears in unchanged altitude, races against us; while he ascends, the lower wings of his machine darkly incline; when he descends, the upper wings shine in

the sun." Curtiss landed with precision, and the sports committee ruled that he had done fifty kilometers in the astonishing
time of forty-nine minutes and twenty-four seconds.

Now it is almost evening, and time for the last flights of the
day. Blériot goes up for the fourth time (about forty meters),
and Rougier, deciding to compete for the Altitude Prize, goes up
at 6:32 in tight curves, surpassing Blériot easily. People are beginning to leave the field, and even Kafka and his friends are
on their way because they have to catch their return train at
Brescia Station, but he ascends higher and higher. The plane
turned, and, as Kafka wrote later, "Rougier appeared so high
that his position could be measured only by the stars which are
to appear any minute now in the sky, turning to a dark color. We
did not cease to turn our heads; still, Rougier keeps ascending
and we drive deeper into the *campagna*." Rougier reached an altitude of 117 meters that evening, but Kafka did not know. While
he and his friends were leaving, in Brescia people celebrated the
achievements of Curtiss and Rougier far into the night, crowd-
ing the Corso, the cafés and trattorias—sufficient reason for a
slow beginning the next morning.

But the fifth day, 12 September, was unanimously declared a
giornata meravigliosa, and after the lengthy celebrations, Italians
and foreigners began to move early in the morning, undeterred
by the traffic jams. Even the elegant people were up early, and a
compact mass of spectators filled the *recinto*, the darker suits of
the men, the red and blue of ladies' dresses, and the light specks
of the many parasols. By eleven, the usual test flights were undertaken by Leblanc, Blériot, and Calderara, but by now these

piccoli voli, little flights, did not attract much attention. In the early afternoon, the competitions started again, and it was Rougier (not satisfied with his record flight of the previous day) who tried, at 2:32 P.M., to challenge Curtiss for the Grand Prize. Unlike Curtiss, however, who flew his fifty kilometers in five continuous and ever-widening circles, Rougier flew in installments, as it were, landing to replenish his gasoline reserve after the first round, and going up for a second, third, fourth, fifth, and even sixth round, being aware that, cruising at an altitude of about twenty meters, he was noticeably slower than the American (Rougier's time was one hour, nine minutes, forty-two and one-fifth seconds, in comparison with Curtiss's forty-nine minutes, twenty-four seconds). Later in the afternoon he competed for the "flying start" race, without success.

Calderara turned out to be the real hero of that grand day, much to the joy of the patriots who had missed him in the lists. After an abortive attempt at 4:35, declared invalid by the referees, he ascended again at 5:45, went up ten meters, and ran the one kilometer prescribed by the Oldofredi, in the excellent time of one minute, fifteen and three-fifths seconds. A little later he was back on the field, encouraged by his success and the enthusiasm of the crowd; he asked his friend Lieutenant Savoia, who had trained with him at Centocelle, to sit on his left, and the plane went up, described a few circles, and landed after two minutes, forty-five and two-fifths seconds, establishing the best time with a passenger on board.

The splendor of the day was enhanced by the arrival, once again, of Princess Letizia and her retinue (by three o'clock there

was less traffic on the Mantua road). She was immediately surrounded by a group of select officials: the mayor of Brescia; the
prefect of police; Conte Oldofredi; Cortlandt Field Bishop, president of the Aero Club of America, who praised the efficiency of
the organizing committees; and, of course, d'Annunzio, always
ready to be photographed with a princess. Her Highness graciously asked him whether he would also be willing to fly, and
his answer (soon to make literary history) was politely evasive,
though he had long ago decided that he wanted to ascend with
one of the famous pilots, preferably Blériot. According to Kafka,
d'Annunzio had "danced" around the hangars like a cat smelling
a dish of sweet milk (to complete Kafka's image), and he had a
friend suggest to Curtiss that the poet would like to go up with
him. Curtiss hesitated, but the sensational Curtiss-d'Annunzio
flight was announced for 5:00 P.M. Curtiss was painstakingly
slow in preparing his biplane, and it was not until five-thirty
that it was rolled out of the hangar, and it was even later when
the aviator asked the poet to sit on his left. It was almost history—the record-breaking aviator from America and the famous
singer of Icarus—but not much came of it. The plane started
"like an arrow," but after a few moments Curtiss landed again,
and d'Annunzio jumped out, enchanted, but a little disappointed, too. D'Annunzio's first flight, if it could be called that
(se così si può chiamare), as the local newspaper said, turned into
legend anyway, and the poet switched to another plane that
evening: Calderara, who understood Italian writers better than
his American colleague did, invited d'Annunzio to go up with
him, and together they went up to ten meters. The poet had his

chance to salute the people on the grandstand who wildly cheered him, "*Evviva d'Annunzio!*" As soon as his feet touched ground again, he gave interviews to nearly everybody about the joys of flying and his urgent wish to become a pilot himself. (Hardly anybody would have believed that only nine years later, he would be organizing an air raid against Vienna.) It was late evening, the shadows were descending on the *brughiera*, and little fires, in the distance, broke through the dark of the night.

CHAPTER FIVE

A New Sensation: *Zodiac III*

SEPTEMBER 13 WAS NOT a good day to challenge the fates, and the committee declared the sixth day of the show a time to rest and to reorganize the services. It even suggested that the suspension of flights might be prolonged until the afternoon of the next day. As a matter of fact, perhaps unforeseen by the sports committee, some of the professional aviators were already leaving, in the manner of traveling divas: Curtiss for Frankfurt and Berlin, Leblanc and Blériot (accompanied by *cavaliere* Mercanti as far as the Brescia station) for France. The airfield was deserted, the press stand empty, the restaurant closed, and the few visitors who had bought tickets for the duration milled around without purpose.

It was the time of the also-rans, or rather of the pilots who had not yet competed and now, hoping to have one last chance, tinkered with their machines, inside and outside the hangars. Moncher, tight-lipped and secretive, had high expectations, not entirely shared by many of his admirers; Cobianchi had returned from Paris with a new propeller, but now the pull of his motor was insufficient; Cagno continued to work on his machine; and the hapless da Zara was busy with his strange *Aerocurvo* model that never made it. Henri Rougier was the only foreign pilot who promised to stay on, and the untiring Calderera, coming by car, hastily surveyed the desolate scene of amateurs and left again in a hurry. Fortunately, the French *Zodiac III* was finally ready to cruise above Brescia and the *brughiera*, and the curious had a sensation to watch.

Conte Oldofredi and *commendatore* Modigliani had been appointed *commissari* to handle the performance of the French dirigible, a great success at Rheims, but they did not know exactly how the airship would fit into the program schedule. On 3 September the special trains from Rheims had arrived in Brescia carrying the deflated and disassembled dirigible along with four monoplanes and one biplane. At the station, ways parted: the planes were carted off to the airfield while the airship was trucked to the Brescia suburb of San Giovanni, where it was placed in a special hangar close to the Società Elettrica e Elettrochimica del Caffaro, a plant that mostly produced caustic soda but also hydrogen to fill the dirigible. Its hangar, compared by some to an aviation cathedral and by others to a huge garage, was a big tarpaulin tent supported by a firm net of iron stays and crossbeams; in front of the entrance, covered by a cloth curtain, was a small meadow of dry grass. Maneuvering space was limited by factories, chimneys, a railway line not much in use, and electrical wires (the power would be cut off whenever necessary).

The committee immediately—and prematurely—announced that the dirigible would undertake regular flights from Brescia to the airfield and back between 8 and 12 September, but the promise was not kept because they had underrated the time needed to inflate the envelope (more than a week), and the commander did not want to take risks while it rained or the wind was strong. In the meantime, rumors were ripe that the Italian military dirigible *I bis* was on its way from Lake Bracciano, near Rome, where it was stationed, but better-informed newspapers believed that it was too early to tell. Experts calculated that the dirigible would have to go either over a 550-kilometer land route or along the Tyrrhenian Sea via Genoa, a journey of 650 kilometers, and it was said that the overland ride was easier but made difficult by the Apennine Mountains; when taking the shore route, the airship still would have to fly over the Ligurian Apennines, and there was also, on either route, the need to replenish the hydrogen and gasoline reserves. There was some confusion about the entire matter; everybody wanted the *I bis* to fly (including the pilots), but Colonel Moris, who was to make the final decision, was attending an aviation exhibition in Frankfurt. Ultimately, military authorities decided that the dirigible was not prepared for the arduous flight as yet. So it happened that the Italian airship never arrived, and the French once more dominated the field.

Only on 13 September was it announced that the French airship had been fully inflated and that Comte de La Vaulx was ready to ascend; on 14 September a curious crowd gathered on the meadow in front of the hangar (entrance fee, one lira), only

to be disappointed because the commander had decided to post-
pone the flight owing to the unstable weather. Among the waiting crowd, Luigi Barzini was particularly impatient; after going
to Rheims, he too had set his mind on flying, but Curtiss had
declined to take him up, preferring d'Annunzio, which left
Barzini frustrated and aching for another chance. At least
Barzini enjoyed excellent coverage by his colleagues from the
press corps, reminding their readers of his many adventurous
trips abroad, on horseback in Barbary, by rickshaw in Tokyo, by
cart in Bombay, and by sleigh in Siberia. They watched closely
when Barzini inspected the airship and its gondola (three seats,
for the commander, the mechanic, and a single passenger), ready
to beat d'Annunzio at the flying game.

On the morning of the fifteenth, everybody was ready at ten,
but the count still hesitated. His little Pirelli weather balloon,
at an altitude of one hundred meters, signaled a windy day, and
it was raining off and on. La Vaulx, who did not want to take
any unnecessary risks, waited until four in the afternoon, when
the clouds cleared up and the sun broke through, before he gave
the order to start. First, the dirigible seemed to go toward Montichiari, but in a graceful curve it veered toward the Brescia Castle, the Piazza d'Armi, and the suburb of San Giovanni, flew
over the center of the city, staying close to the Duomo, and
slowly returned to the hangar, where it landed forty minutes
later, the landing ropes handled by soldiers and mechanics. The
landing was noisily applauded by the spectators, who for good
reason admired the count's skillful pilotage between the electric
wires. By 6:15 the *Zodiac III* was safely inside its hangar again,

and the press eagerly compared the event to the fictions of Jules Verne.

The next day, La Vaulx was ready to fly his airship to the aerodrome and back with Luigi Barzini as his passenger of honor. The day was sunny and calm, and thousands of enthusiasts, inside and outside the hangar, waited to see the ascent, scheduled for 10:00 A.M. But the *bersaglieri* platoon to handle the ropes did not show up—"for excellent reasons," Barzini reported, because they were eating breakfast at the barracks. The airship had to be towed out of the hangar by amateurs, among them, on the port side, Orefici, the mayor of Brescia, and on the starboard side none other than maestro Arturo Toscanini, who had come from Milan with his wife; an airship was never handled by more elegant gloved hands and more select personnel, wrote the reporter.

By eleven the count—with Barzini (finally) in the narrow gondola together with a jolly mechanic named Legall (who was killed in a freak accident only a few months later) and many green sacks of ballast and dangerous canisters of oil and gasoline—gave the necessary orders, and the dirigible rose to an initial altitude of fifty meters, passed the cemetery and the railway station, and then at four hundred meters began to cruise at an average speed of forty kilometers per hour toward Castenedolo and Montichiari. Barzini experienced a brief moment of claustrophobia and vertigo in the gondola, given the empty space below and the body of the airship above; he imagined himself, somewhat theatrically, falling through the emptiness; and yet he enjoyed himself tremendously on a "minuscule planet," as it were, "living the impossible." He watched the little people on farms, the cars that stopped on the roads, everybody gesticulating; he felt almost as if he were returning to his childhood, overcome by an emotion that was "quiet, profound, and sweet."

When the *Zodiac III*, flying the Italian tricolor next to the French flag, turned a noble curve around the airfield, people applauded and cheered wildly, and then the airship solemnly disappeared again to return to the Brescia hangar. On the way back, Barzini noticed a cluster of buildings with new red roofs, people dressed in white, and still others indifferent (he thought) to what was going on in the sky. It was the insane asylum, where the patients lived on in their own inner "world of fantastic visions," where everything was improbable anyway.

For the landing, the *bersaglieri* were ready (after lunch), and when he stepped out of the gondola, Barzini was as enthusiastic, if not as gushy, as d'Annunzio had been about his first flying experience. It was, Barzini reported in a full-page article in the *Corriere della Sera* on 17 September, "an incommensurate parenthesis of dreams in the middle of life . . . a time of ecstasy from which it was difficult to wake up." Yet even the extraordinary was turning into a kind of routine; by 5:15, the commander was ready for a short trip over the city again and invited *commendatore* Modigliani, of the committee, to join him in the gondola. By 6:00 P.M., the *Zodiac III* was back at the Brescia aerodrome, where its return was graciously welcomed by Princess Letizia, who had arrived just in time with her lady-in-waiting and social secretary. From now on, La Vaulx's trip from Brescia to the airfield and back was a feature on the regular program (except, possibly, on 17 September, when it rained again).

The airship appeared just in time to make people gasp, gossip, and admire, but down below, the days were rather slack at the aerodrome. Without most of the international professionals, the public's often rather skeptical attention turned to the five Italians who were still competing, and news was not encouraging. The personnel on the steam train threatened—in a statement that many considered rude—to go on strike during the final days of the *Circuito*, not to protest against the Belgian management but because they felt mistreated; at times, their own compatriots had bodily attacked conductors when there wasn't space available in the overcrowded trains. On the airfield itself, a group of journalists gathering around a hangar were challenged by overly efficient guards, the journalists and guards fought, and not only with words, and the committee had a difficult time assuaging the mutual ire.

At least Calderara made an attempt on the evening of the fifteenth to compete for the twenty-kilometer prize, invited Savoia to be his passenger (not in the rules), and ascended easily. But after a few turns over the *brughiera*, the motor failed, and Calderara had to glide to a landing after completing only nine kilometers. Next day it was Cagno's turn: he went up for the first time in his Voisin biplane, but after only forty meters or so, at an altitude of twelve meters, his machine took a nosedive and crashed, the pilot escaping unhurt from the debris.

The forty-eight hours preceding the Grand Finale were nothing to write home about, and the journalists, *faute de mieux*, substituted interviews for hard news. It rained off and on, Curtiss's hangar was used as a garage, Cobianchi moped in his, and Anzani, whose machine had been damaged when it had to be dragged off the airfield (his propeller was destroyed hitting the hangar walls), simply and resolutely gave up. He distributed parts of his machine to other flyers, which enabled Cagno to patch up his own plane with Anzani's fuselage and undercarriage, which had remained intact. Guido Moncher, so tight-lipped and inscrutable behind his ornate full beard, turned out to be a nice and even an affable guy, after all; in a longish interview, he talked about himself as captain of the Trento Voluntary Firefighters and as owner of a bookbinding shop and a small printing press. Moncher explained that he had high hopes for his *elicoplano*, though he had not come to break any dangerous records, for the simple reason that he had *la sua famiglia* back home. It was not the best time for Barone da Zara's home-built "Bat," either; it moved only a few meters and then refused to budge any more (perhaps the time for homespun flying machines was gone altogether). Yet there was still some hope for the competitions to come. Henri Rougier, traveling in Verona and France, let it be known that he was definitely prepared to go for a new altitude record, challenging Latham's 155 meters at the Rheims *Semaine*.

The Brescia *Circuito* had been planned to show what Italian aviators and builders of flying machines could achieve in international competitions, and during the days of the Grand Finale, 19 and 20 September—which at that time were also national holidays commemorating the fall of the pope's secular power and the elevation of liberated Rome as capital of a unified Italy —politics and sports, not for the first time, combined in the minds of the spectators and journalists. The presence of King Vittorio Emmanuele III, many members of the government, and delegations from both houses of Parliament enhanced the public splendor. The nineteenth was again a *giornata meravigliosa*; after rain almost all night, the air was fresh, with a whiff of autumn and mud on the ground. Traffic built up early and the first flights commenced at ten o'clock. Barone Leonino da Zara, who had not done much so far, tried to ascend with his big "Bat" machine, but without success (the undercarriage stuck in the mud); the machine had to be dragged to the hangar again, and many spectators invaded the restaurant for an early snack. The unfortunate baron tried his luck again when the ground was dry, but again in vain.

It was clear that Calderara, the Italian naval lieutenant, and Rougier, the French professional, would fight it out, and ultimately the Italian patriots had their day. The young and elegant Rougier was ready on the runway at 3:20 P.M. for a first test of the engine; after nearly three hundred meters on the ground, he went up easily and firmly, turned a wide circle over the *brughiera*, and landed again, greeted by the warm applause of the public who had taken him to its heart. Calderara, with Savoia at his side, went up twice: once at 4:15, rising easily but forced to land almost immediately when the machine veered dangerously to the left; and once again at five o'clock, definitely going for the *Corriere della Sera* Prize (twenty kilometers). The plane quickly left the wooden tracks (it was a Wright machine that had to be catapulted), rose to fifteen meters, and, the motor working perfectly, cruised over the field until the spectators lost sight of it over the Porro homestead; Calderara returned, in perfect balance, to repeat his feat and landed after a second circle, everybody shouting *"Evviva!"* The referees confirmed that, having done the distance in twenty-one minutes, forty-three seconds, he was the hero of the day. In the meantime, *Zodiac III* had come and gone on its regular flight, and after six o'clock, Cobianchi, untried as yet, and da Zara brought their machines out of the hangars but could not get off the ground. By that time spectators were leaving the field, with cars, trams, carts, and bikes, jamming the narrow roads, and the committee's well-meant recommendation that car owners use the minor road via Ghedi merely added to a traffic congestion that was already worse than ever.

CHAPTER SIX

The Grand Finale

IN THE EARLY-MORNING hours of 20 September, attention shifted to the Brescia railway station, where the king was to arrive at eight-thirty to spend a busy morning in the festive city before going on to the airfield in the afternoon. In the great hall of the station, where now immigrant West African commuters wait for their Milan train, generals, prefects, select civil servants and bank managers gathered. Places of honor were reserved for Prime Minister Giovanni Giolitti and four cabinet ministers, among them V. E. Orlando. As soon as the locomotive signaled the coming of the king, the music band of the 74th Infantry Regiment intoned the "Royal March" and the soldiers on guard snapped to attention. The king, in dress uniform and adorned with all his medals, was welcomed by Mayor Orefici and Senator Federico Bettoni, and the crowd of more than a hundred distinguished people moved to a grandstand near the station, where the king was to witness the unveiling of a monument to

Giuseppe Zanardelli, famous Brescia liberal and former chief of government.

The monument, designed by the gifted Piemontese artist Davide Calandra, was attractively modern in the best sense, creating its own space: it had as background a stone wall showing an ancient quadriga and, in front, Zanardelli speaking, as it were, to an attentive audience. (The artist could not have foreseen that Zanardelli is now facing the via Antonio Gramsci, named after the founder of the Italian Communist Party.) Speeches by Senator Bettoni, the minister Cocco-Ortu, and Mayor Orefici (who quoted Josuè Carducci) were appropriately dignified. After the unveiling, the king briefly visited the Palazzo Bettoni, went on to an industrial exhibition at the castle and an arts show, and, at noon, returned to the Bettonis, his Brescia hosts, for an intimate luncheon. Meanwhile, the mayor welcomed members of government, generals, magistrates, and the artist Calandra at an official city luncheon of their own, where it was announced that the king had donated twenty thousand lire to be distributed among the poor of Brescia.

Back at the airfield, people enjoyed a clear day, and though there was little flying in the morning, early preparations were made to welcome the king in a special *loge* of the grandstand, adorned with many flowers, and a special detachment of *bersaglieri* was in attendance. Some tinkering was going on in the hangars, but Moncher was melancholy; in an engine test he had broken his propeller, and there was little hope that the damage could be repaired in time. At 10:50, Rougier, on a test flight, ascended to a height of fifteen meters, but the engine did not work regularly and he decided to land again. Parking spaces were filling up rapidly, a military band played, and carabinieri were posted at all entrances.

At 2:45 the flag was hoisted announcing that the king was coming, but his cavalcade of three automobiles stopped at the wrong entrance and had to be redirected. By then, Calderara had gone up for his first afternoon flight in the machine the French had put at his disposal. He rose almost vertically from the tracks and immediately crashed with a loud thud, damaging the runners and a few fittings. Fortunately he had his own airplane, entrusted to him by the Aviation Club of Rome, prepared for further flights in the later afternoon.

Shortly after 4:20 the king and his entourage visited the hangars, where Oldofredi and Mercanti introduced the aviators to His Majesty—melancholy Moncher, Cobianchi (rather relaxed, in fatigues), Cagno, Calderara (whom the king had met before), and Barone da Zara, who promised to fly later (he failed again). People were ready for the finale of the *Circuito*, and they were not disappointed. At five o'clock, Calderara, in his uniform, chain-smoking as always, announced he was ready to go for the Grand Prize (fifty kilometers) in his own machine; a little later he was catapulted into the air and ascended elegantly and firmly. At an altitude of about fifty meters he began his first wide curve over the *brughiera* (time, ten minutes, nine and three-fifths seconds), followed by a second one (ten minutes, three seconds), and, encouraged by frenetic applause, a third (nine minutes, fifty-two and one-half seconds), fourth (nine minutes, fifty-two seconds), and fifth. People waved handkerchiefs, hats, and parasols, the infantry music played on, and when Calderara landed, the referees confirmed that he had been only one minute slower (fifty minutes, fifty and four-fifths seconds) than Curtiss (forty-nine minutes, twenty-four seconds).

A contemporary Rebus Motor advertisement.

The rest of the afternoon was pure drama and a good deal of chaos. While Calderara was still circling over the *brughiera*, impatient Rougier (who had tested his machine once again at 4:00 P.M.), went up again "like an eagle," the reporters said, and calmly and in concentric circles removed himself to an ever-increasing altitude. Calderara had by now descended, and the king was congratulating him with a handshake; he then had to leave for a dinner at the Palazzo Bettoni and a gala performance at the Brescia opera before catching his train later that night. Many people had left with him, and they missed the moment when the referees came running from their obervation post and shouted that Rougier had reached an altitude of 198.5 meters, breaking all

previous records, those of Latham at Rheims (155) and Orville
Wright in Berlin (172, though not officially registered). Later in
the evening the mayor of Brescia invited the pilots to an official
dinner. Luigi Barzini, in a speech as political as it was *sportif*,
toasted the "sister nations" France and Italy. It was a pity that
Curtiss, who had performed so well, had already left for Berlin.

The committee published the following list of prizes and awards:

1. Grand Prize of Brescia (50 km distance)
   First Prize L30,000   Glenn Curtiss   49 minutes,
      24 seconds
   Second Prize L10,000   Mario Calderara   50 minutes,
      50 and ⅘ seconds
   Third Prize L5000   Henri Rougier   1 hour, 9 minutes,
      42 and ⅕ seconds
2. International Modigliani Prize (altitude) L5000
   Henri Rougier   198.5m
3. International Passenger Transport Prize (at least 9 km
      distance)   L3000
   Mario Calderara, with one passenger   18 minutes,
      8 and ⅕ seconds
4. Flying Start Prize (100 m/l km)
   First Prize   Glenn Curtiss   8 and ⅔ seconds
   Second Prize   Alfred Leblanc   9 and ⅔ seconds
5. Oldofredi Prize (1 km)
   Mario Calderara   1 minute, 15 and ⅗ seconds
6. *Corriere della Sera* Prize (20 km)
   Mario Calderara   21 minutes, 43 seconds

The King's Cup was awarded to Calderara for his splendid fifty-kilometer performance, and the Royal Gold Medal went to the engineers Buzio and Restelli for their Rebus motor, used by Calderara, Rougier, and Moncher.

CHAPTER SEVEN

Puccini at the Restaurant

THE ORGANIZING COMMITTEE of the Brescia Air Show was, I assume, pleasantly surprised when Giacomo Puccini, world-famous heir to Verdi, made his appearance among the prominent spectators, and later observers may derive a special pleasure from noting that his visit to the aerodrome exactly coincided with that of Franz Kafka and his friends. Puccini's press coverage was far less impressive, however, than that of Gabriele d'Annunzio's, whose presence the journalists celebrated even more clamorously than that of the king himself.

Puccini's trip to Brescia may have been totally improvised, and yet, perhaps, it was foreseeable to many. People realized that the well-received performance in Brescia of *Madama Butterfly* on 28 May 1904, soon after its scandalous flop in Milan on 17 February, had opened the opera's way to the international world, including London, Budapest, Paris, and New York, so the composer had reasons to visit friendly Brescia again. Others, knowledgeable about his private habits, knew that Puccini was a technology fan and spent a good deal of money, certainly considerably more than he did in support of his poor relatives, on motorboats (he had five) and, especially, on elegant and racy cars—always, of course, driven by a discreetly uniformed chauffeur, very much visible in all photographs. There is not much evidence that Puccini attended the pioneering car races of Brescia, but he was a man enchanted by speed; between 1901 and 1908 he bought six expensive cars, among them a De Dion, an early Lancia, a Phaeton-LaBuire, and another six-cylinder Dialfa Lancia; between 1910 and 1924, the year of his death, he acquired eight vehicles, including a Harley-Davidson motorcycle with a sidecar and, in 1922, a luxury car for ninety thousand lire.

Puccini was the first famous musician ever involved in a car accident, and the aftereffects of the mishap were to affect the lives of his family, and not only them, for many years to come. On 3 January 1904, Puccini, Elvira (not yet legally married to him), their teenage son, and their driver left his hometown, Lucca, on a rainy night; not far from town, the chauffeur miscalculated while taking a sharp curve, and the car overshot a little going downhill, fortunately not overturning but coming to a halt sideways. The woman and the boy were unhurt, but the driver broke a leg and Puccini his left shinbone. He was carried, rather dramatically, on a flatboat to his villa of Torre del Lago; biographers do not tell us about the injured driver, whose name was Guido Baruglia. Treatment was old-fashioned. Puccini spent months in bed and in a wheelchair and complained endlessly, especially to his London friend Sibyl Seligman—as Elvira, her sister Ida, and his own widowed sister Nittiti scurried around to keep the household going. "I am in a prison," he wrote in a letter to his London correspondent, who was always ready to listen to his problems, marital or musical.

It was at that time that Elvira hired a young girl from the village, Doria Manfredi, as a kind of nurse to the invalid, who seemed to have only *Madama Butterfly* on his mind. The Manfredis were badly off; the father had died, Doria's mother had to fend for herself and several children, and though people in the village were aware of Elvira's lack of virtues as a *padrona* (she unhesitatingly mistrusted all servants) and of Puccini's amorous adventures, the young girl accepted the job. The village was right: Doria later found herself in an inescapable web of conflicts and suspicions, and committed suicide; Elvira and Giacomo's relationship, only recently fully legalized, nearly fell apart; and Puccini tried to escape from his home, which had become a "hell," as far away as London and as close by as Brescia.

Let us tell the melancholy story step by step and in its complete context. In early January 1904, Elvira's husband, whose bed and board she had left in 1885 to live with the poor musician Puccini, passed away, and Elvira and Giacomo, less compatible than they ever suspected, were thus free to marry. In his prolonged convalescence after the car accident, Puccini decided to end his longish affair with Corinna, an intelligent Turin law student whom he had met on a train, and Elvira wanted to use her rare chance (though Corinna took her love letters to a lawyer and there was talk about blackmail).

In late September or early October 1908, Elvira, as passionately jealous as ever, began to suspect Doria, by now an attractive young woman, of immorality. Puccini, as usual, protested his total innocence, but Doria was given immediate notice and left disconcerted, because she believed that she had been serving loyally and well. Puccini himself, who could not stand Elvira's fits of jealousy, bolted and, always a good traveler, went off to Paris and London, later meeting Elvira in Milan to talk things over, but to little avail. Matters went quickly from bad to worse.

Elvira believed that Doria and Giacomo were trysting late at night, after Doria finished her ironing and he was still working in his studio, and she donned men's clothes to catch the lovebirds at the lakeshore (in vain). As Puccini confessed to Sibyl, he did meet Doria once or twice secretly (one hopes, to assure her of his support), and he wrote a reassuring letter to Doria's mother. Elvira, true to her petit bourgeois origins, never mustered the courage to confront Giacomo's mistresses of higher social standing or intelligence, but Doria was another matter, and the *padrona* was heard publicly declaring in the village that Doria was "a slut, a tart . . . a whore," and, as sure as there were Christ and Madonna, she, Elvira, would drown her in the lake. Elvira even turned to Doria's mother and to the village priest and demanded that Doria be expelled from the village.

Doria, who adored Puccini with childlike devotion, felt betrayed by the world and did not know what to do. She took three pills of a potent disinfectant and died in atrocious agonies, five days later. In an almost Sicilian turn of mind, she may have wished, on her deathbed, to be medically examined to prove her innocence. The authorities, for their own reasons, insisted on an

autopsy, and the village doctor, a friend of Puccini's, signed a
certificate that she died *virgo intacta*—exonerating Puccini and
shifting all the blame on Elvira, who made haste to flee to Milan;
her husband believed that she would have been lynched by the
villagers if they had caught her at home. Doria's brother, in true
folklore fashion, first wanted to kill Puccini and then, after the
doctor's testimony, Elvira. And it was he who, backed by village
opinion, prompted his mother to make a legal deposition accus-
ing Elvira of defamation of character resulting in suicide.

The police prefect of Viareggio, in turn, passed the papers on
to the court of Pisa, and the date for Elvira's trial was set for
July 1909. Doria's family amassed many documents, including
old school records, to demonstrate her unblemished character.
Elvira's lawyers were inept and negligent, to say the least, and
the court found Elvira, in absentia, guilty on three charges,
defamation of character, slander, and "menace to life and limb."
She was sentenced to five months and five days in prison, a fine
of seven hundred lire, and payment of all court costs. And, of
course, it was expected that the Manfredis would press civil
charges against her. The sentence was a terrible blow to Elvira
and to Puccini; their son Tonio, no longer a teenager, ran off to
Munich and wrote to his disconsolate father that he wanted to
emigrate to Africa.

The appeal Elvira's lawyers presented on 24 July 1909 did not
show a high level of legal sophistication. They argued that, unfortunately, Elvira had listened too closely to what her relatives
had said, and that Doria was (anyway) a hysterical girl; they also
wrote, rather condescendingly, that Elvira's threat to drown Do-

ria in the lake could not be taken seriously by anybody in the
village because Lake Massaciuccoli was extremely shallow and
even a child would have to wade quite a ways into it before coming to deep water. The press entertained its eager readers with
daily reports of this scandal, and Puccini, who intermittently
returned to Torre del Lago, tried valiantly to limit damages and
to reestablish for himself a kind of life that would make it possible to continue working on his new opera, *La Fanciulla del West*.
He offered the Manfredis twelve thousand lire to quash the civil
suit. The Manfredis accepted the money (actually, one-twelfth
of Puccini's annual income at that time) and built themselves a
new house and a tombstone to Doria, to which Puccini, it was
said in the village, brought flowers every year. He also traveled
to Milan to meet Elvira a few times on neutral ground. She remained adamant at first ("always the same violence," he remarked), but finally broke down and accepted his views and
demands. The couple moved to the Bagni di Lucca and later to
the fashionable spa of Montecatini to repair the marriage, but it
was not at all easy. Every word had to be considered carefully,
and Puccini began to travel restlessly again, unable and unwilling to stay at home for more than a few days. Meanwhile the appeal was pending, and it was uncertain whether Elvira would
have to serve time, ignominiously.

PUCCINI CAME to the air show at Brescia by way of Milan, and
it may have been a last-minute decision. The organizing committee had welcomed guests and tourists with a festive evening

concert of the Corpo di Musica Municipale, and I assume that a composition by Puccini would have been included if the committee had known he would come, unless people were shocked by the recent events at Torre del Lago and the disgrace of the Puccini ménage. The concert program, as performed on 3 September, included *I Vespri Siciliani* (Finale, Act IV) by Verdi, the national hero, Rossini's *Guglielmo Tell* overture, the prologue to *Mefistofele* by Arrigo Boito, and a popular waltz.

Puccini arrived at Brescia only on 9 September, inevitably competing for the limelight with Gabriele d'Annunzio, who made his first appearance at the same time. Kafka and Brod noticed Puccini early on, and the *Sentinella Bresciana*, recording the presence of many famous Italian artists, devoted much fanfare to the poet and briefly interviewed Puccini, who preferred to stay at the restaurant, "far from the masses," surrounded by his friends. The reporter, who called himself Scudo, reminded his readers that the *grande musicista* was an important man as well as a shy one (occasionally true) and that he sought refuge in the restaurant in order to avoid press people and their "Kodak" cameras—"naturally," he added, as if Puccini, after the recent scandals and the sentence still hanging over Elvira, did not have a special reason to sidestep too many questions.

Puccini first shared a late breakfast with a group of reporters close to the *Provincia di Brescia*, who noted that he talked little about flying but a lot about music. He was quite expansive, discussing the differences between oriental and occidental, German and Italian music. The conversation inevitably turned to Wagner, whose compositions, Puccini said, had "a solid and exuberant complexity"; one needed, he added, "unusual physical stamina" to listen to them. One reporter, evidently wanting to please the maestro, somewhat irreverently remarked that it would be best to listen to the first act of an opera, go for a walk, perhaps take a bath (*fare magari un bagno*), and then listen to whatever was being played when you returned. Puccini, not to be outdone, confirmed that he had never felt more deeply about Wagner's music than one evening in Rome, when he arrived late at the opera and heard the orchestra intoning the first bars of the third act of *Die Walküre*. When asked about his own compositions, he began to speak about *La Fanciulla del West*, on which he was working; his only "sport" in recent months, he remarked, was composing, that is, putting melodies into the soul and heart of his *Fanciulla*. This was not exactly true, because he had been unable for months to concentrate on his opera. Dodging questions, he went on to explain his idea about his American heroine, Minnie, "a simple girl living in a virgin country, among honest people," and he added that, in theater, "he had always studied that passion which vibrates by a rather instinctive force and without those psychological complications that come from our sophisticated, *raffinata* society." The American West, he explained, corresponded to something substantive in his own nature, "a land almost empty where people lived, dispersed in the solitude of the grand prairies." Yet the shy musician was also his own best public-relations man (perhaps with a view of d'Annunzio, the other superdiva, prancing around with the famous pilots), and he reminded his audience and the reporter of the success of *Madama Butterfly*, launched to the world at Brescia. "A

thousand performances in America alone, and now a new contract for thirty-five weeks in sequence, everything in English!"

Did he want to say something about flying? Unfortunately
the committee had just raised the green flag (the winds were too
strong, no flying), and Puccini responded appropriately enough,
saying that flying was, here and now, "a sport of patience, at
least for the time being." Even the local reporter had to admit
that the weather was awful, clouds descending and the fog rising
from the *brughiera*, and he wished that Puccini might have a
chance to blast his glorious music from his American opera to
blow away the clouds and to stop the winds. At least he was
more patient than the spectators, who were beginning their
whistles in a chorus of protest; it took two more hours before
the committee gave the order to hoist the white signal flag (flying, perhaps). Fortunately, Puccini could not know that in another corner of the airfield, Princess Letizia, talking with
d'Annunzio about prominent people who wanted to fly, skepti-
cally remarked that Puccini surely was not among them because
he was too heavy, *troppo pesante.*

Kafka and his friends watched closely, and though Kafka's re-
mark that Puccini had an "alcoholic's nose" may have been a bit
of caricature, his friend Max Brod, the opera lover, was more
personal. "I love Puccini because his inventions have been often
helpful to me, as if coming from divine reason." He was aware of
the unusual moment, and walked around him and observed the
face of the great man "with the prominent, perhaps even thick
nose, and his reddened cheeks."

It is a different question altogether why Puccini and d'Annunzio almost studiously avoided each other at the air show, or at least did not give the assembled journalists a chance to speak or write about them together. It was not that they did not actually know each other. As early as 1894, Puccini had hoped that d'Annunzio would be willing to write him a suitable libretto, but d'Annunzio demanded too much money, as usual. Yet the prince of poets and the composer went on hoping that one day they would collaborate on a splendid opera. In 1900, d'Annunzio visited Puccini at Torre del Lago to discuss the story of Count Ugolino, who betrayed the pro-emperor Ghibellines and, a little later, a story about a medieval astrologer. But Puccini did not like distant historical material, and d'Annunzio did not want to write strange and decorative stories. In April 1906 they met at a fashionable Florence hotel to prepare a contract: d'Annunzio would deliver a libretto for an advance of twenty thousand lire, twenty percent of the theatrical income, and fifteen percent of the print sales. But, again, d'Annunzio did not deliver the prospectus promised for the end of May, and Puccini, who had developed a rather unexpected liking for the proletarian Maxim Gorky, did not approve of d'Annunzio's romantic plans for an opera called *La Rosa de Cipri* (The Rose of Cyprus), of all things. A year later, d'Annunzio was again offering his poetic services to Puccini, again they met to discuss ideas of mutual interest, but again nothing came of the conversations.

Puccini and d'Annunzio had each come to Brescia for different reasons—Puccini because he loved fast cars and motorboats and, mostly, to run away from home, d'Annunzio because he was long interested in the technology of flying and dreamed about

the Icarian, not to say superhuman, potentialities of mankind.
They never were to collaborate. Puccini visited d'Annunzio in
France, but he did not like the poet's idea of an opera about the
Children's Crusade. The nascent Italian film industry and the
war did the rest. D'Annunzio wrote scripts for the early, pioneering blood-and-sandals movies (three in 1912), and when
Italy declared war on Austria, the rather unpolitical Puccini
thought about his many friends in Vienna and Munich (especially about his Bavarian mistress, Baroness von Stängel, who
succeeded in moving to Switzerland), while d'Annunzio, enthusiastic about the war, was, by his own wish, transferred from the
Novara Lancers to the Italian Air Corps and was able to attack
the Austrians across their airspace with heroic bravado.

Puccini continued to acquire high-speed cars, and once went
on a three-thousand-kilometer automobile trip through south-
ern Germany and Switzerland. At a new villa in Viareggio, he installed up-to-date technical gadgets, including a radio (1921), an
electric gate opener, and an automatic sprinkler in his garden.
He even considered a short trip by plane. When he was staying
in Vienna in 1923, living high in that impoverished city, he
planned to take a plane hop to Budapest. His son Tonio declined
to go with him (preferring to stay in Vienna with a local Mizzi),
and the aging father did not want to go alone. A few biographers, including the knowledgeable Mosco Carner, believe that
Puccini's creative forces went into decline after the tragic death
of Doria Manfredi, who reappears only in his last opera, *Turandot*, in the disguise of Liù, the beautiful young slave. Liù confronts the merciless Turandot (Elvira), *di gel cinta*, "enclosed in

ice," bravely endures torture, and kills herself rather than betray her love, *segreto et inconfessato*, a gift to her master, *un dono al mio Signore . . .*

I cannot agree that Puccini's *Il Trittico* or, especially, *Gianni Schicchi* or the unfinished *Turandot* demonstrates a diminished power of musical invention. It is possible that Puccini's crisis was caused not by the shock of Doria's death and his deep regret about it, but by his artistic encounter with the music of Arnold Schönberg, Igor Stravinsky, and Richard Strauss, and growing doubts about his own gifts. Art and life are rarely bound to each other in a way that can be described easily. Puccini was certainly saddened by Doria's death, but he also enjoyed his prolonged on-again-off-again sexual affair with Giulia Manfredi (1915–21), who waited on tables at her father's trattoria, where Puccini liked to drop in for his minestrone, or rowed him across the lake when he went after waterfowl. As letters and postcards show, they both enjoyed the time they had together, and when Giulia (not closely related to Doria) was later interviewed by a reporter from *Oggi* and was asked whether she had known Puccini, the eighty-year-old woman almost laughed. "Oh, boy! Did I know Puccini!" Thus my rendering of her *"Accidenti se l'ho conosciuto!"*

CHAPTER EIGHT

Kafka and the "Air Dogs"

K AFKA'S ARTICLE about the air show, written during the last two vacation days at Riva, was published on 29 September 1909 in the Prague *Deutsche Zeitung Bohemia*, a daily newspaper of nationalist and liberal leanings with first-rate pages of literary entertainment and cultural information. Paul Wiegler, himself an erudite critic, edited the feuilleton, and he was certainly justified in cutting nearly one-fifth of Kafka's original text, especially the part that described the trip to Brescia and the dirty lodgings. Wiegler wanted to give the reader a chance to hear more about the actual events, at least those of 11 September—a slow day, bad weather, and yet some unexpected and marvelous performances by Curtiss and Rougier toward evening. Kafka, the cub reporter who had never written a newspaper article before, did not want to sacrifice his personal attitudes, his special imagery, or his almost obsessive interest in physiognomy and gesture, however. The resulting text is unbalanced, nicely flowing, and yet with sudden knots and eddies, and the after-breakfast readers may have been disturbed by the unusual turns that militated against easy perusal—for instance, Kafka's glimpse of amputated "beggars who had grown gigantically fat in their little wheelchairs," stretching their arms across the tourists' path, or his description of Italian cavalrymen "hopscotching" over the field, a willfulness of participle later absent from his lawyerly prose. He was someone from Bohemia who had just spent a few days at Riva, an enclave of sunshine and palm trees, and that may explain why he called the *brughiera* "an artificial wasteland" arranged in an "almost tropical region."

Kafka's report about Brescia is a unique text that moves between the exigencies of the newspaper genre and his own nascent habits of writing. His reporter speaks in the first person plural (he explains that his "we" consists of the triple "I" of the group); only rarely, in dramatic moments on the airfield, does he suggest that his and his friends' viewpoint melts into the impersonal one of all the spectators: Blériot ascends, "and we stand down there, pushed back and nonexistent [*wesenlos*]." The sensibilities of the three friends combine to create a collective individuality confronted with the Other, the different world of Italian sounds, language, and behavior; and when Kafka's reporter tries to apologize, as it were, for the habits of "us," the assumptions and inclinations of tourists from the Austrian lands distinctly emerge. (A few years later, the friends, above all Max Brod, would have insisted that they came from Prague's Jewish community, but not yet in September 1909.) In the deleted initial paragraphs of the article, the reporter confesses to being aware that a kind of anxiety faced "the Italian organization of

Die Aeroplane in Brescia.

Von Franz Kafka (Prag).

Wir sind angekommen. Vor dem Aerodrom liegt noch ein großer Platz mit verdächtigen Holzhäuschen, für die wir andere Aufschriften erwartet hätten, als: Garage, Grand Büfett International und so weiter. Ungeheuere in ihren Wägelchen fettgewordene Bettler strecken uns ihre Arme in den Weg, man ist in der Eile versucht, über sie zu springen. Wir überholen viele Leute und werden von vielen überholt. Wir schauen in die Luft, um die es sich hier ja handelt. Gott sei Dank, noch fliegt keiner! Wir weichen nicht aus und werden doch nicht überfahren. Zwischen und hinter den Tausend Fuhrwerken und ihnen entgegen hüpft italienische Kavallerie. Ordnung und Unglücksfälle scheinen gleich unmöglich.

Einmal in Brescia spät am Abend wollten wir rasch in eine bestimmte Gasse kommen, die unserer Meinung nach ziemlich weit entfernt war. Ein Kutscher verlangt 3 Lire, wir bieten zwei. Der Kutscher verzichtet auf die Fahrt und nur aus Freundschaft beschreibt er uns die geradezu entsetzliche Entfernung dieser Gasse. Wir fangen an, uns unseres Anbotes zu schämen. Gut, 3 Lire. Wir steigen ein, drei Drehungen des Wagens durch kurze Gassen, wir sind dort, wohin wir wollten. Otto, energischer als wir zwei andern, erklärt, es falle ihm natürlich nicht im geringsten ein, für die Fahrt, die eine Minute gedauert hat, 3 Lire zu geben. Ein Lire sei mehr als genug. Da sei ein Lire. Es ist schon Nacht, das Gäßchen ist leer, der Kutscher ist stark. Er kommt gleich in einen Eifer, als dauere der Streit

31

Franz Kafka's newspaper article about the airplanes of Brescia,
in the Prague newspaper Bohemia, *29 September 1909.*

such undertakings." He implies the traditional Austrian belief that Italians are incapable of efficient administration, and he underrates the grace of the Italian gift for improvisation. When the friends arrive at the Brescia station, where "people screamed as if a fire burned under their feet," the friends half ironically vow to stick together in that alien scene, come what may, and the reporter asks himself whether they had not arrived, in fact, with a kind of enmity [*mit einer Art Feindschaft*]. It is a pleasant surprise that the people at the committee offices completely ignore "their inner malice, as if it did not exist," and yet feelings of belonging to another country return when the reporter notices that Guido Moncher, from the Austrian Trento, flies the Italian and not the Austrian flag as he should. (When Italy entered the war against Austria in mid-May 1915, Kafka wrote in his diary that he went on a pleasant walk to the Prague suburbs, and in a brief sentence noted with regret that he would be declared unfit for army service because of his heart problem. He wanted to escape the office routine to another kind of life.)

The tourist perspective of Kafka's reportage does have certain advantages, especially in contrast to the overwriting by the local press, and people and events emerge in a new light when seen from his distance. The hangars seem to him "like closed theaters of roving comedians," and the "suspicious little wooden contraptions" in front of the aerodrome, toiletlike, surprise people with an unexpected sign, GRAND BUFFET INTERNATIONAL. Kafka reveals some of his true interests when he observes faces and how people move: Rougier, "a little man with a striking nose," running back and forth in shirtsleeves; his wife in "a tight white dress, a little black hat strongly pushed into her hair, her feet delicately placed apart in a narrow skirt"; heavyset Blériot, "his head firm on his neck," immovable in his pilot's seat, and around him his assistants, "as if all were dreaming"; the "long ladies of today's fashion," forced by their corsets to walk rather than to sit; and Curtiss reading his American newspaper, slowly, in his hangar. At times it appears that Kafka, that fond lover of early movies, was interested more in human physiognomies and expressive body language than in airplanes and their competition.

Yet Kafka the reporter has a sharper eye for technological detail than does his friend Brod, who, in the manner of the impressionist, dwells lovingly on the colors of gloves, but can hardly handle technical detail. Kafka is the insurance writer who has learned how difficult and dangerous machines can be, especially in the construction business (the subject of his first published insurance report), and almost professionally has a good deal to say about engines, propellers, wings, and the mechanics' teamwork. Of course, his perspective is limited by his expectations: it is clear that the friends came to Brescia to see, above all, the famous Blériot (about whom Brod had written an earlier article), and though it may be true that Blériot's many false starts on the afternoon of 11 September attracted much attention, Kafka's concentration on Blériot actually camouflages the pilot's less-than-successful performance. Kafka's belief that Blériot was flying "the historic machine" in which he conquered the English Channel was simply mistaken (though it was a plane of the same type). Nevertheless, the long passage describing how Blériot and his crew tried to start it up exquisitely describes the interplay of men and machine—the attempt to set the propeller in motion (working and stopping again with its own cunning), the shift of attention to the engine, oiling its points, the careful and selective tightening of screws, getting a spare part that doesn't entirely fit and has to be worked on with a hammer, right in front of the hangar. Few people have written about Blériot, I believe, with greater loyalty to the nitty-gritty job on the field.

Kafka's similes work together effortlessly to deprive the aviators of any heroics and larger-than-life stature, in absolute contrast to d'Annunzio's attitude, and their performances, even those on the brink of making new records, are pulled down from the skies to the homely and civil world of school and office. Other writers of the time, among them the Futurists or science fiction authors, insisted that aviation was something radically new, threatening, or revolutionary, but Kafka's images are curiously reductive, including the one of a plane irresolutely moving on the runway like a clumsy fellow (*ein Ungeschickter*) on the dance floor. The most conspicuous example compares Blériot's motor, which does not work in spite of every effort, to a hopelessly stupid, stubborn lad in school: "the motor is merciless, like a kid, helped by everybody, the whole class prompts him on what to say, but no, he cannot do it, again and again he gets stuck, again and again he gets stuck [the repetitions are Kafka's], on the spot, he fails." Rougier, ascending to record altitude, appears to sit at his levers "like a man at his writing desk," which can be reached "behind his back with a little ladder"—the grotesque touch anticipates the absurd office condition of the authorities in *The Trial* and creates the impression that the aviator, up there among the stars, by a stroke of the pen has been taken down to a branch office of a Prague insurance company. He is not among d'Annunzio's winged supermen.

The reporter keeps his eye firmly on "the wide field" (*das weite Feld*, in German: he is surely quoting a key phrase, implying the vicissitudes of life, from Theodor Fontane's novel *Effi Briest*), and his rare lines considering what it means to fly were unfortunately cut by the Prague editor. Again, it was Blériot who captured the reporter's imagination, and looking at his small airplane (*eine Kleinigkeit*), he wonders how the pilot will manage to go up. People who move on water, he remarks, have an easier time; they first can try puddles, ponds, rivers, and ultimately the sea, but aviators have to cope with an elemental either/or; to them there is only the air and then "only the sea." Kafka enters Blériot's sensibilities: "he will fly now, nothing more natural," and yet his ideas about what is natural (*das Natürliche*) inextricably combine with "the concurrent, general feeling of the extraordinary that cannot be kept away." Kafka never liked psychological analysis, but his insight at least anticipates our own feelings when we are fastening our seat belts, trying to ward off an awareness that we are in an ordinary and yet, considering the uncertain elements, extraordinary situation. I wonder what Kafka thought about Brod's idea that an air show should be arranged somewhere else too, perhaps in Prague; it would be financially rewarding for potential investors, he believed, to invite one of the star aviators to Bohemia for a show, if not for a competition. Brod returned to his idea two years later in a novel, but Kafka, who mentioned this business suggestion in the concluding lines of his article, never brought it up again.

In his pioneering book about literature and aviation (1978), the Swiss poet and scholar Felix Philipp Ingold discussed for the first time Kafka's article about the Brescia air show. He suggested that on the *brughiera* and watching Curtiss nearly disappear on the horizon, Kafka observed a "process of miniaturization" that he turned into an essential metaphor of changing into something small (*ins Kleine*) and of disappearing without a trace (*ein spurloses Verschwinden*). People may achieve self-realization only by making themselves as small as possible, Kafka thought (possibly like the ancient Chinese, Ingold remarks); and it is not really necessary to quote from Gustav Janouch's rather uncertain conversations with Kafka that he held the belief that moving to disappear created a chance for self-loss and fortunate self-realization. The question remains, however, whether it is possible to read early Kafka in the light of his later views. I would rather look at Kafka's imagery about flying, about human and other beings, above all horses and dogs. I may run the risk of insisting on crisscrossed meanings and sets of irreconcilable ideas, but I suspect that Kafka simply thought that, for a number of reasons, flying was not appropriate for human beings caught in the Piranesi prisons of their lives.

Some of Kafka's early prose pieces—usually gathered under the title *Beschreibung eines Kampfes* (Descriptions of a Struggle)—are a quarry of situations and motifs, later developed individually, but it is also true that his "untrammeled fantasies," as Ingeborg Henel has called them, so visible here, are soon pushed aside or disciplined to a more translucent functionality. The first part of the narrative, if it is one, brings together a young man who prefers reticence and a casual acquaintance of his who wants to talk expansively about his feelings; in the course of a night walk through the city, clearly Prague, as denoted by specific monuments, churches, and streets, the reticent one (the I-speaker) constantly tries to sympathize and yet to escape, and in a moment of particular irritation, he throws himself into the air to enjoy more fully the calm light of the moon. It is so easy to "swim" through the air, without pain or effort, and "I did not do that ever before!" He notices his annoying acquaintance "down below," and "with a new stroke" rises above the bridge railing and cruises around the baroque statues of the saints; unfortunately, he does not fly high enough above the pavement, his eager acquaintance grasps his hand, and he is pulled down to earth and to further irritations. The Charles Bridge flight vision goes back to 1904–5, that is, a few years before Kafka actually watched an airplane flying, and it is noticeable that his narrative of flight above the bridge and the river does not lack an ironic dimension. The young man, who is of Kafka's age, speaks matter-of-factly, Icarian heroics of d'Annunzio's brand are totally absent, and he even confesses that his exercise in levitation was, at least partly, a literary affair. He was seeking a higher altitude because he feared that people would say his flight was not worth being narrated (*nicht des Erzählens wert*).

Lonely among the writers of modernity, Kafka liked to renew ancient fables of the animal world, and it is a strange experience to read what he has to say about horses and dogs, not to mention storks, a marten in the synagogue, star singers who belong to a nation of mice, and a burrow in his subterranean realm. Early on, his storytellers watch fairy-tale horses fly through the air, as do the police horses in *Der Kaufmann*, 1907–8 (The Merchant) or the cavalry in *Kinder auf der Landstrasse*, 1908 (Children on a Country Road); and I wonder what his observant Eduard Raban, in *Hochzeitsvorbereitungen auf dem Lande* (Preparations for a Country Wedding), has in mind when he admires, in an urban scene without any automobiles, "the bodies of two horses that flew horizontally as if catapulted." The sentence contains a strange coincidence, in the original German, of the terms *fliegen*, *wagrecht*, and *geschleudert*, all used by others to describe how a Wright airplane began its flight—catapulted and then moving fast along a runway of wooden tracks before rising in the air. Yet Kafka wrote Raban's lines in 1907, two years before he had a chance to see Wright's catapult or Calderara's plane (so much for positivism).

In the story *Der Landarzt*, 1916–17 (The Country Physician), horses are turned into magical animals of incredible power, strength, and speed, "densely steaming bodies" that transport the reluctant physician (who would rather stay at home to defend his servant girl against the vicious attack of a stableman) to another village where they need his help. "The carriage is swept away, like wood in a torrent," the physician feels but a "piercing whir" and finds himself, instantly and without knowing what has happened to him, in the other village. Mephistopheles's magic horses in *Faust* inevitably come to mind.

In contrast to the flying horses, Kafka's "air dogs" (*Lufthunde*), or rather the analysis of their exploits in *Forschungen eines Hundes* (Researches of a Dog), has attracted many readers and learned interpreters who, involved in their task, often forget to laugh at these prose pieces as much as Kafka did when he read them to his friends. In "Researches of a Dog," a late narrative (1922), much is at stake—the possibility of knowing, the isolation of the individual mind alone in humanity or in his (Jewish) community, the function of scholarship going beyond accepted beliefs, the glorious revelations of music (foreign to Kafka). The "air dogs" endlessly challenge the researcher, who himself happens to be more or less an ordinary dog, or so he says. They *are* puzzling; and although the narrator has never seen any, he shares the astonishment of dogdom about a fellow being that simply hovers in the air without any means of sustenance, gladly suffers the atrophy of its legs, does not procreate, and yet is happy up there, "alone, self-sufficient." These "air dogs," if they ever walk, merely take a few prancing steps, as if in deep thought, and compensate for the absurdities of their life, the narrator has been told, by "an almost unbearable babble." Dogdom does not know what their existence means; interpreters in the human sphere have ingeniously suggested, among other possibilities, that they stand (hover) for the artists who want to differ from society, or for Western assimilated Jews who have alienated themselves from authentic Judaic tradition. Kafka seems to be reminded of himself (the isolation of the inquiring intellect), and in his parody of canine research the inquisitive dog moves in a world without human beings, food comes from above or rains down in response to particular gestures and dances. The "air dogs" are, we may assume, lapdogs minus the lap that remains invisible to the researcher's eyes. Yet, to complicate matters even further, the *Lufthunde* remind us, linguistically, of the Yiddish *Luftmenschen* (air people), who do not have any regular means of income, who swindle, brag, and, in general, are not considered good candidates for marrying a nice daughter with a good dowry. I am convinced that Kafka, master of self-deprecation, thought of himself as a *Luftmensch*, but that does not exclude the possibility that his parade of air dogs, so irritatingly close to air people, tells us what we may think of the new flying breed in their machines.

Kafka's characters, the narrator included, never soar freely, and they always run up against somebody or something that blocks their way, be it snow on the way to the castle, a hermeneutic gatekeeper, or entire hierarchies defending the law. You move, as it were, by inches; and if certain strange beings on the brink of life, like the hunter Gracchus, whistling Josephine, or the cryptic Odradek, may *glide away* into self-negation and, perhaps, fulfillment, other, more ordinary beings cannot, and should not, move too easily. They may have the illusion, as the imperial messenger does, that "if there would be an open field, how would he fly," but space itself, suddenly a forbidding system of hindrances, rises against him, chambers, staircases, courtyards, palaces, and "again staircases and courtyards; and again a palace, and so forth through the millennia . . ." Even the silly "Bucket Rider" (*Der Kübelreiter*), freezing in the winter cold and riding his big pail like a Pegasus to the coal shop around the corner, does so in vain. He cannot buy what he needs, and, riding higher and higher (as confirmed by a paragraph in Kafka's first copybook), ultimately lands in arctic isolation on an empty planet of ice. "People who limp believe they are closer to flying," Kafka warns in an aphorism, "than people who walk."

It is possible to argue that young Kafka indulged more easily in momentary visions of flying, overcoming the boundaries of gravity and space, than did the later author, who viewed any attempt to rise above the earth (that home and prison of everything alive) with suspicion and misgiving. Yet Kafka never wanted to be a philosopher, unlike his friend Max Brod, and it would be foolish to substitute a catechism of his ideas for the confusing presence of his imaginative prose. His vision of throwing himself into the air and swimming above the Charles Bridge still has ironic innocence (1904–5); and in his prose piece "The Merchant" (1907–8) another moment of elevation occurs, at least in the optative. A frustrated merchant, caught in his daily business, on his way back to his apartment opens the door to the elevator, pushes the button, and feels the beginning of a new freedom. The stair bannisters glide down behind the glass planes of elevator, "falling like water," and the merchant rises in a liberating motion. In that moment he not only speaks his own thoughts, burdened so long with business worries, but wishes to enjoy all the possibilities of life: "fly away [*flieget fort*], your wings, which I have never seen, should carry you to your native valley and to Paris if you feel that you should be there!" It is the last time that flying has the glorious power to liberate and to fulfill secret wishes. Kafka's counterimage clearly emerges from a nightmarish fragment (written before October 1917), a bloody, brutal event told by a soldier who has orders to take a town beyond a swamp (he may be Egyptian, considering the battle cry

"Kehira! Kehira!"). Much has been destroyed, corpses and yellow smoke block the gates, but the soldier, or commander, eager for spoil, leads an attack through the side streets, hacks a door to pieces with his axe, and finds himself face to face with a strange old man—strange, because the old man has long (archangelic?) wings, on their outer rim higher than he is himself. The astonished invader asks the old man why he and his like did not use their wing power to escape. The town elder responds with counterquestions that may imply many of Kafka's views. "We should fly away from our own town? Leave our homes? Our dead and the Gods?" A *Luftmensch* may have chosen to escape, but not a human being aware of his own moment in history, his place on earth, his ancestors, and his ritual responsibilities. Reading this fragmentary narrative in the age of the Shoah, I cannot help feeling that it is one of the most tragic, if not suicidal, that Kafka ever wrote.

CHAPTER NINE

Max Brod Changes His Mind

M AX BROD NOTED that Kafka was eager to go from Riva to Brescia to watch the pilots, but he may have more than welcomed his friend's wishes because he had just written a little two-page piece on Blériot and his glorious crossing of the Channel, published in the Berlin periodical *Die Gegenwart*. It must have been composed between 25 July 1909, the day of Blériot's feat, and 29 August, when the Berliners watched a zeppelin flight, as described in another article following Brod's. His piece was a meditation about fate and the loneliness of the triumphant pilot, in which he lyrically contemplated the many articles and photographs that had appeared after the Channel crossing made Blériot overnight the most famous pilot in the world, fervently welcomed by huge crowds in London and Paris. These were poetic thoughts, triggered by media reports that Brod had seen in the press and wanted to share with his readers—Blériot in front of his monoplane; two gentlemen leaning against the plane (rather strange); Blériot's serious face, con-

fronting the infinity of the sea and the sky; his austere aviator's dress, actually reminiscent, as Brod suggested, of an opera
Mephisto or an operetta *Fledermaus* ballet, with the smart
leather cap covering much of his cheek and all of his forehead.
Brod did not like the usual comparison of Blériot's plane to an
insect, but reluctantly accepted it for the time being because it
alluded to the plane's complexity (*Unübersichtlichkeit*), which
had something unclassifiable about it, without any real unity of
shape. He only narrowly avoided the insect image in his report
about Brescia, however.

The short piece in *Die Gegenwart* reminds us that Brod was, in
his earliest publications, a gifted lyrical poet, not only a writer
of sentimental novellas, and he had little difficulty reviewing before his adoring eyes the incisive moments of the historic day in
late July when Blériot flew from Calais, or rather Barraques, to
Dover. Brod reflects on how the plane was transported by train
to Calais, lifted carefully from the carrier, and moved to the
shore, where it was covered by a tent. He is deeply moved by a
famous snapshot showing Blériot and a friend, Blériot indicating
the future flight path with a walking stick. Blériot utters the final commands, rises, and by now "is alone like a sick man in his
bed," everybody else far and distant, the loyal mechanics and a
few elegant, well-turned-out ladies with huge hats (ladies' fashions being one of Brod's special interests). People always wanted
to know when Blériot was happiest, and Brod, too, ponders the
question. Was it when the pilot discovered Dover on the horizon, or later, when he passed over a torpedo boat, or when he felt
himself to be the only human being between the earth and the

sky? Not to speak of the moment when he was welcomed in London by masses so closely serried "that a train could have run over the surface formed by their straw hats"—a wonderful surrealist image closer to Kafka's writing habits than to Brod's at the time.

The gifted Max Brod was nothing if not ambitious, and he submitted his report about the events in Brescia first to the *Neue Rundschau*, the best of the German literary journals going back to the end of the nineteenth century. Only when its editors declined to publish it did he send it on to the Berlin periodical *Die Gegenwart*, where it was printed without further difficulties in March 1910. About Brescia he wrote in a different mode; if, in the Blériot meditation, he moved close to his lyrical poetry, in the Brescia piece he again assumed the role of the fashionable, cosmopolitan man-about-town (forget the dreary Prague post office where he had to work) and wrote in the manner of his sentimental and erotic novellas that had found admiring readers at home and among the Berlin Expressionists. He had for years been reading a good deal of Schopenhauer, and he did not see any reason why he should be overwhelmed, *nil admirari*, by the new sports spectacle of the flying machines. Unhesitatingly he pretends that he spent days on end at the airfield, "from morning till evening," starting out every morning anew to watch the events, that he feels "used to everything," including the fashionable lunches that he enjoys together with all other refined participants in the grand restaurant. I am certain Brod did not have enough money to pay even for a simple menu, and I believe him

only when he says that he enjoyed a glass of refreshing Aranciata
in the heat of the day.

Brod wants to make his readers believe that he is attending a
newfangled sports event and, taking his cue from the wooden
structures on the field, speaks about the vast "turf," the "hippo-
drome" (*Pferderennplatz*) of Brescia, and often pushes his horse-
racing metaphor by saying the hangars were erected where the
paddocks usually were, or, for a change, compares them to the
boathouses of a rowing club, well known to him and Kafka from
the Vltava River. He cannot hide his aesthetic interest in atmo-
sphere and color; he writes impressively about the yellow wood
of the hangars, hot in the sun, describes the vista as "grayish
green" or the forest as "milky and bluish" (*bläulichmilchig*) on
the horizon. Kafka had briefly noted the presence of soldiers in
their unusual regimentals (at least to Austrian eyes), but Brod
cannot refrain from closely watching the movement of the cavalry, the infantry, and a detachment on bicycles—the Milanese
cavalry with little red pompoms on their eighteenth-century
hats, the white dust rising from the hooves of the horses, and
the cyclists with strange kerchiefs protecting their heads and
shoulders against the glaring sun, reminding the opera buff of
the Egyptian priests in *Aïda*. We have shifted for a while, he
says, half-ironically, to a military drilling field, and the father-
land wants its share.

Both Kafka and Brod had keen eyes for the shapes and secrets
of ladies' dresses (Kafka had written a pensive piece about the
fit of dresses and the woman's body before going to Brescia),

and Brod gives more space to the aristocratic ladies of Rome than to the aviators. He believes that the dresses on parade are nearly identical, of impeccable shape, curiously "armored" down to the knees, so that the upper part of the body is left soft, pliable, and bending "over a firmer foundation, a second ground." The unvarying silhouette prompts the women to wear immense hats at a courageous slant (with only part of the face visible) and extraordinary accoutrements, for instance a strawberry-colored waistcoat, with long black ribbons and heavy metal buckles in the back. It is the conformity of the elegantly correct dress, Brod remarks, that makes the ladies greet each other with such feverish embraces and theatrical kisses— they want to prove that they are two, and not one! Yet he greatly admires the *beau désordre* of which the women themselves may be unaware, and he lovingly dwells on the little irregular folds at the seams of the long jackets, "square shadows, tiny lights, creases caused by long automobile trips," the last trace of un-fashion allowed. Brod reports less about how the famous men are dressed: Puccini, about whom he knows much more than Kafka does, wears spats and homespun trousers, and d'Annunzio a "majestic cravat" (he also has a circular mud spot on his white pants and a blue thread on his shoulder). I do not believe everything that Brod has to say about d'Annunzio; he undermines his credibility by asserting that he sees the poet "often these days," calls him a "second king of Italy," and tells us what d'Annunzio has to say to the journalists about his new aviation novel, or what he cites from his "Icarus" poem. Here, Brod is simply quoting from the *Sentinella Bresciana*, which the friends read at Riva.

Brod's reporter likes to think of himself as a "habitué of the turf" who cannot be surprised by any new spectacle, and, given this self-assigned role, it takes considerable time before he yields to the excitement of an unusual day and to feeling "a strange, pure joy" as he watches, in the last sunlight of the day, flights of extraordinary courage. "Invisible hands," reminding him of a spiritist séance that he attended before going to Brescia, raise the curtain of a hangar and reveal Rougier's airplane. He knows he should be astonished by a machine that has been invented only after many false steps, and yet he cannot feel too excited— after all, it just looks like a "threshing machine," and the dust swirling is like chaff rising from a barn floor. Again, the image sounds reductive, perhaps intentionally so. Considering Brod's distance from the rural world of peasants, wheat fields, barns, and threshing, however, the extended comparison still retains an irritating element of something not entirely known and certainly not easily integrated with the blasé reporter's customary, exclusively urban experience. He comes close, at least implicitly, to the bird metaphor (which he disdained in his Blériot article) when he tells us now that Blériot's monoplane "suddenly lifted its tail" (*der Monoplan lüpft seinen Schwanz*). He may use the trite image merely to indicate his ambivalent perception of how natural it seems to fly (seeing the plane rise), almost a déjà vu perhaps originating "in dreams"—and yet, "if you observe a plane that does not go up [like Leblanc's] you are immediately con-

vinced that flying is impossible," the airplane standing there in
the field like "a forgotten booth at a country fair." He experiences a rapidly changing awareness of what is natural and what
is inconceivable, but ultimately, watching Rougier and Curtiss,
all doubts, details, and trivia are forgotten, and the reporter
feels intoxicated "with courage, and the awesomeness of a new
time." His last glimpse is of Curtiss after his record performance. "I only watched the man go by, limping, tired, with a
stoop . . . his face tender and full of energy, all at once."

IT IS NOT surprising that critics are fond of pointing to Kafka's
article about Brescia, and yet it is equally if not more instructive to ask what his friend Max, a major Prague author of the
German language and a Zionist author of note, remembered
about the *Circuito*. Brod does not make it easy to trace his devel-
oping literary and ideological attitudes. He wrote much about
his own life and work, magisterially sketched a definite image of
himself, and was, from early on, skillful and rather categorical in
interpreting his own ideas and those of his friend Kafka as he
understood them. In the first decade of the century, it was his
personal and political struggle slowly to discuss and assert his
Jewishness and to come closer to a particular Zionist solution of
the Jewish question. (Martin Buber's ideas of Jewish culture
were closer to him than Theodor Herzl's territorial commitment.) Since he was always inclined to describe his progressions
from a later point of view, he preferred to explain the changes
in his sensibilities and thoughts from a philosophical vantage

point, as a movement of ideas, rather than to contemplate the metamorphoses of his fictions corresponding, whether he wanted it or not, to the evolution of his beliefs. The truth is, unfortunately, that he takes a dim view of his early fictions and creates his personal canon by stressing the importance of his later novels, from *Tycho Brahes Weg zu Gott*, 1916 (Tycho Brahe's Path to God), to *Stefan Rott, oder das Jahr der Entscheidung*, 1932 (Stefan Rott, or the Year of Decision), which inevitably prompts his interpreters to pass lightly over his early productions, including *Ein tschechisches Dienstmädchen* (A Czech Servant Girl), *Jüdinnen*, (Jewish Women), and *Arnold Beer: Das Schicksal eines Juden* (Arnold Beer: The Fate of a Jew), with their erotic affairs, chic society, and fashionable sports, including a few Brescia reminiscences. It is precisely in the novel about Arnold Beer that Brod leaves behind the world of the dandy and turns to a lasting affirmation of Jewish traditions, family bonds, and a metaphysical commitment as his future way of life.

Most readers would agree that Brod began, in a hesitant and often contradictory process, to grasp the importance of his Jewish origins in the three or four years following his Brescia excursion, radically changing his self-perception. By 1910, Brod still believed that he lived in a city of two nations, German and Czech, and classed himself among the German writers, but within a few years he was convinced that three nations were there, German, Jewish, and Czech, and he considered himself a "Jewish writer of the German tongue" (1913). Brod's short novel *A Czech Servant Girl* definitely marks a stage in his development; it is one of many Prague German novels telling us about a

young German, often a student or white-collar office worker,
who falls suddenly in love with a buxom Slavic girl (always
lower-class) in a rather condescending affair in which the young
man does not learn much about the girl's people, though he hon-
estly tries. Brod's William, who comes from Vienna, does not
even see that his lovely Pepitchka is on the run from her husband, a brutal raftsman from the Podskal suburb; she kills herself in the end.

In the divided, or rather triple city, Brod's story was not welcomed eagerly. Milena Jesenská's more famous aunt Božena, a society novelist of the Czech middle class (in Jaroslav Hašek's
Good Soldier Švejk, a literate lieutenant, in an ultimate act of criticism, uses pages from her novels as toilet paper), declared that
Brod's novel was offensive to her nation because Brod only acknowledged the physiological shape of Czech womanhood, and
young Jewish readers were astonished that the third nation was
totally absent from the city. Leo Hermann, writing in the *Selbstwehr* and representing the Zionist orientation of younger Jewish
intellectuals, said that he was impressed by Brod's resolve to
work for the reconciliation of the nations, but added that such a
rapprochement could not be achieved in bed alone. Fortunately,
novelist and reviewer met shortly thereafter, and Hermann, of
the Zionist Bar-Kochba Club, told Brod something about the
fundamentals of Jewish life and history then and there.

By 1910–12, the young lawyer Brod had come to take Martin
Buber's ideas about a new Jewish consciousness seriously, went
to see the performances of a traveling Jewish theater troupe (together with Kafka, but with far less enthusiasm), attended

meetings of the Bar-Kochba Club, and often visited his philosophical mentor Hugo Bergman (later a librarian in Jerusalem), who in turn recommended to him that he read Theodor Herzl's novel about returning to Israel. So far, the novelist Brod had only once sketched the portrait of a Jewish character, but rather indirectly. In his *Castle Nornepygge* (1908), Herr Pollodi, an arbiter of impeccable fashion (anticipating Thomas Mann's Chaim Breisacher in *Doktor Faustus*), reveals by faint traces of Yiddish syntax in his speech that he comes from a ghetto and overcompensates with an artificial aura of good breeding for what he feels to be a social predicament.

In *Jewish Women* Brod renews the genre of the spa novel, instituted by Jane Austen and Walter Scott, and squarely confronts the contemporary Jewish middle classes of his origins—though Bohemian Teplitz, the playground of the Prague Jewish bourgeoisie, offered less elegant establishments than did Bath or Cheltenham. A young student ready to fall head over heels in love for the summer season does not know whether he deplores the fate of the attractive Irene, who came to the spa with her mother to catch the right husband, or feels for sturdy Olga from the provinces, strong but lacking in refinement. Everybody wants to be terribly genteel; parents discourage "Jewish behavior" in their children (whatever that is), a few Yiddish idioms are suppressed, and ideas of Zionism are discussed. Perhaps echoing an earlier review in the *Selbstwehr*, Kafka did not particularly like this novel; he did not know what to do with the student as storyteller, and at a time when Zionism had come to galvanize the discussion of possible solutions to the Jewish question, the writer (unfortunately) did not suggest his own viewpoint in the text. In alluding to Brod's novel, Kafka uses the term "Zionism" for the first time in his writing (*Diaries*, possibly 27 March 1911), and it is ironic that the purveyor of so many meanings accuses his friend of offering less than one.

Brod has told us in his later autobiography (1960) that he definitely did away with his Schopenhauerian, ethically indifferent, and (merely) aesthetically committed younger self when he killed off Walder Nornepygge in his novel of 1908. However, Nornepygge's bored attitude certainly reappears in the voice of the Brescia reporter and, ultimately, in the figure of Arnold Beer, who (fortunately) goes through a change of heart. Brod himself once suggested that the death of his grandmother was a brief episode in his rediscovery of Judaism, and in the novel, her presence alone—down-to-earth, impetuous, and rooted in an older world of Yiddish and religion—forces Arnold to make a decision that will transform his life forever. The first sixty or seventy pages of *Arnold Beer: The Fate of a Jew* are among the best Brod ever wrote because he sees himself, as a dandy, with loving and ironic eyes, and the small world of the Prague assimilated Jewish *jeunesse dorée* before the First World War (and a few years thereafter) has never been illuminated with greater accuracy and puzzled distrust—the changing groups in school, on the *corso*, at the tennis courts, ballrooms, cafés, rowing clubs, and horse races. In this closed sphere people much admire Arnold, who thinks of himself as a "unique personality" making himself attractive to many friends by imitating their interests without really having a central interest of his own. (As far as women are concerned, he of course knows his way around red-light Prague, but he is too much of an egotist to care for more than quickly passing affairs.) No wonder that Arnold and Walder Nornepygge, artfully resuscitated by the novelist from the earlier novel, do not like each other at all. Walder thinks Arnold is rather crude, and Arnold, for his part, believes that Nornepygge is a conceited fool. One is the mirror image of the other.

It is Arnold's rich friend Phillip who asks him what he thinks about Blériot, Brod's hero, and praises the wonderful achievements of recent aviation: "the Wright brothers went up in their plane to considerable altitudes, Zeppelin was successful on his first trips, Blériot crossed the Channel." Phillip promotes Brod's idea about the magnificent business possibilities he had impressed on the hesitant Kafka upon leaving the *brughiera*, and he does not find it difficult to convince Arnold how important and profitable it would be to invite Blériot to Prague or, if Blériot refuses, one of his friends or disciples. For entirely different reasons, Arnold (who thinks of his public image) and Phillip (who thinks of his pocket) immediately organize a committee of local notables to raise the needed funds; Arnold, hoping for something that will heighten his experience, accepts the committee's presidency (a far cry from Brod's cheap ticket in the *recinto*), deals with the delegations from the suburbs who offer open space for an aerodrome, discusses transport facilities with the railway administration, reviews questions of law and order with the police, writes a long and confused article about the advances of aviation from Icarus to Brescia, and establishes his own office in one of the new hangars (exactly corresponding to those at Brescia) near a little spa close to Prague where the show is to be held. In his brain, "ideas rolled like avalanches of stones," the narrator somewhat ironically remarks, and Arnold begins to believe in "the immense synthesis of life" and a path to a "future, sparkling and stormy." Unfortunately, Blériot declines the invitation, the record aviator Farman is busy elsewhere, and the committee settles on Monsieur Ponterret, a third-rate Belgian who has built his own plane, imitates the chain-smoking Latham (Blériot's competitor), and, the novelist assures us, belongs to a passé "aviation period of childish stammer" (*eine Kinderstammelperiode*). Ponterret, though honest, is not lucky; on his first try the plane does not start, and on the eve of the show, a wing breaks off and spare parts have to be ordered from Paris. The show is postponed, but in contrast to Brescia, where the committee revalidated all tickets if there was no flying, Phillip (who is deeply in debt) refuses to return any monies, and Arnold begins to grasp that he has been manipulated by his greedy friend. Discouraged and humiliated, he seeks a way out—as far away as possible.

Arnold Beer's voyage, short on the map but long spiritually, leads to another dimension of life and time. He accompanies his mother to the bedside of his ailing grandmother in a small place in northeastern Bohemia; and if Brod, in the early pages of the novel, modifies the fin de siècle novel, close to Thomas Mann, in the second part he confronts Arnold, linguistically and culturally, with Jewish tradition surviving more strongly in the far-away village than in the city. Arnold expects his grandmother to be in her death throes, but the old woman, frail, caring, and indestructible, enjoys the visit of her favorite grandson, though he has considerable difficulty understanding what she says because she speaks a Silesian village idiom according to Yiddish syntax and rich in Yiddish vocabulary. It is a historic moment of a particular kind. For the last time, in a Prague novel written in German, Yiddish resounds and reminds us of the older language used by Prague and Bohemian Jews from the eleventh to the mid-nineteenth century, after which they switched to German or Czech. The old woman, though weakened and ill, appears to Arnold a Jewish Deborah, feisty, willful, full of fighting spirit, almost savage. Her powerful presence casts a shadow over everything he has experienced so far, and in a sudden turn he decides to abandon his empty life, society, turf, and the air show (a failure anyway), his haphazard affair with a north Bohemian *shikse*, and in a sudden shift of interest resolves to explore his Jewish past. He sees his forebears as Maccabean warriors; his grandmother's impetuousness reminds him of an Ur-Jewish "heritage of the biblical rage with which a people resembling predatory animals pushed across the Jordan to destroy the towns of unknown tribes by the keenness of the sword." Yet at the same time he feels the softer side of the ancient Jews, "their plaintive songs, like the rustling of the wind in a forest, their natural habit of leading and telling stories, their forthright way of living." Leaving his grandmother behind he goes off—a sudden Zionist—to Berlin, at that time a great liberal metropolis, where he wants to take up the Jewish cause in the newspapers immediately.

The question whether Brod knew Božena Němcová's novel *Babička*, 1855 (Grandmother), the beginning of modern Czech prose, when he was writing *Arnold Beer*, is worth considering, even though it is difficult to arrive at a philologically convincing answer. Both grandmothers, the Jewish and the Czech (quite apart, though living in nearby regions of Bohemia), direct their grandchildren, unsure about their future, to discover to which people they really belong. Němcová's grandmother, of a poor weaver's family, by her example, her folktales, and her (Czech) wisdom, guides her granddaughter Barushka—against the wishes of her mother, to whom a German education means social advancement—to an enlightened and vital knowledge of her origins, so much so that the young *Fräulein*, reared on German penny dreadfuls, turns into Božena Němcová, the first Czech woman writer of importance. But we still do not know whether Brod read Němcová; the German Slavicist Walter Schamschula examined the teaching programs of the Prague Stefansgymnasium, where Brod was a student, and found many Czech poets there, though not Němcová, but I find it improbable that the popular founder of Czech prose was entirely missing from the pedagogic repertory of that elite school. In Brod's novel, Arnold's Lina tells him about the young girls in her village who, on early-spring mornings, go to the brook to wash their faces and hope for more beauty; this folktale appears in Němcová's *Grandmother* and may be shared by Bohemian Czechs and Germans. It is perhaps more important that *Grandmother* was a favorite novel of Kafka's, who modeled a few minor characters and situations in *The Castle* on it. Since Kafka read the novel as early as 1902 (as Hartmut Binder suggests, with hesitations about the date), it is not impossible that Brod learned about the Czech grandmother from his friend.

I think there is another reason to reconsider young Brod's relationship with his Czech neighbors in town, especially in light of Arnold Beer's enthusiasm for the new heroes of aviation. I do not wish to accentuate Brod's isolation on Prague's Jewish-German island in the Czech sea, because I know that Brod, more than many of his friends, was interested in Czech painting early on, at any rate in the Czech members of the supranational Osma Group, and Czech music (not to speak of what he later did for Hašek and Janáček). But, writing *Arnold Beer* for a German audience, he found it difficult to look beyond the interests of his readers. Arnold Beer, with the connivance of his author, tries to organize a Brescia air show in Prague, discusses the qualifications of the new international aviators, and totally ignores the contemporary feats of the first Czech pilots right under his nose. He is well informed about Blériot, Latham, and Paulhan, but he does not seem to know anything about Jan Kašpar, a Czech engineer who, by 1909, had begun his experiments and, after he had bought a Blériot plane and an Anzani motor, went up on an army drill field at Pardubice, not far from Prague, for twenty-five meters and two minutes. (He preferred the early morning because later in the day infantry was training and cows grazed.)

On 19 June 1910, Kašpar went up in a first public performance, and on 14 and 15 August (at the time when Brod was writing his novel) attracted 100,000 people to the Prague suburb of Prosek (now a subway station), who came to see what he could do. Among the witnesses of his flights was the young actress Božena Láglerová, who decided on the spot to become a pilot, went with her mother to Germany to the Gerke school of aviation, and received her diploma on 9 November 1911 as the first and only woman among the ninety-one certified aviators in Germany and Austria-Hungary. (Harriet Quimby, the first U.S. aviatrix, was certified three months earlier, on 1 August 1911, and fell to her death eleven months later.) Láglerová crashed once, and impatiently joined an aviation troupe that performed in the United States, Cuba, Haiti, and Santo Domingo, where the organizer of the group absconded with all the funds. When war broke out, she wanted to join the new air corps, but the old emperor declined her application. She married and settled down, and I wonder what she thought about the German Luftwaffe planes over her hometown when she died in 1941. To say more about her adventures and frustrations would require another book.

CHAPTER TEN

A Dirge for Otto Brod

O F THE THREE Prague friends who visited Riva and Brescia, Otto Brod, the youngest, was not at all eager to write
a report for the newspapers. As a self-appointed expert on the
Lake Garda region, which he had visited in 1908, he wanted to
enjoy his brief vacation and duly went on to the air show. Both
Max Brod, four years his senior, and Franz Kafka, who praised
his eye (*scharfes Auge*), keeping apart the different types of airplanes, liked to ask for his advice when they scribbled away on
their articles and appreciated his impartiality. A good time was
had by all, and in the following year, on 8 October 1910, the enterprising three went together on vacation to Paris; unfortunately, Kafka developed a furunculosis, returned after ten days
to Prague, and left the two brothers to enjoy cafés, monuments,
museums, cinemas, and, inevitably, houses of ill repute, on their
own.

Max and Otto's feelings of being inseparable went back to
childhood days, when they had spent many summers on the

shores of the Baltic Sea at Misdroy, perhaps not the most elegant of places, with their irascible mother (the father had to stay on in Prague at his job as a bank accountant). The brothers, together with other kids, roamed the beaches, played the piano and violin in the music room of the modest Kurhaus, and conspired to protect the inarticulate Czech servant girl who had been hired to do the cooking and cleaning against the ire of their mother and the injustices she inflicted in an almost predictable ritual (the mother had to be confined to a psychiatric institution later). In his novel *Der Sommer, den man sich zurück-wünscht*, 1952 (The Summer That Should Return), Max Brod movingly remembers how happy he was with Otto, "who felt a gift in himself to do good" (*der die Gabe in sich fühlte . . . das Gute zu tun*), in the long summers, sharing their love for music from the Romantics to Bizet. There were moments of jealousy, but nothing could really disturb their love for each other.

In World War I, Otto served as an officer in the Austrian army, and the peace-loving Max particularly admired him for his resolve to bring home in the fall of 1918 an entire artillery regiment against the orders of his superior officer. In a kind of Caporetto in reverse, he guided the regiment home from the Isonzo, via Belluno and Toblach, to its base at Wiener Neustadt, without a single man missing, "past horrible heaps of dead horses, destroyed automobiles, field pieces and mortars stuck in the mud." (The quotation is from Max Brod's novel *Dei Frau, nach der man sich sehnt* [The Woman You Desire].) Max believed that Otto had "undone the war," at least at the spot where he had found himself. Yet it is difficult to know more about Otto's life as entrepreneur, husband, father, musician, and writer in the late 1920s. The brothers moved in different walks of life, meeting occasionally at cafés or at the opera or, perhaps, at the popular Prague weekend places, as for instance Lake Jevany, and Max was particularly enamored of Otto's daughter Marianne, who early turned out to be a talented singer.

Loyal friends and family members, Jewish and non-Jewish, were brought closer to one another when, in the early 1930s, Hitler's Germany began to threaten liberal Czechoslovakia, and it is probable that Max increasingly encouraged Otto to write and to publish. Otto Brod's novel *Die Berauschten*, 1934 (The Intoxicated), written between the summer of 1932 and March 1933, was published by a small firm in Vienna but printed in Holland, and it can be read, even after seventy years, with considerable intellectual pleasure. Otto writes in the confessional mode, often dominating in his brother's novels, about the sad experiences of a man of forty who falls in love with a self-willed woman whose erratic behavior he cannot understand, at least not initially; only after many twists and turns, happy skiing days in the mountains, fashionable tango dancing in Prague nightclubs, an unsuccessful suicide attempt and an overdose, it turns out that the young woman hopelessly depends on morphine. Trite phrases abound, especially when the narrator speaks about his nights of passion, but Otto Brod inserts, in the manner of Thomas Mann, who once ceremoniously praised this novel, a number of timely discussions, e.g., a trenchant critique of Mozart's *Magic Flute*; a surprisingly modern defense of a market economy that cannot work when the state constantly interferes; and a discussion of communism being something for the angels or for ants.

In 1938, Max Brod's novel *Abenteuer in Japan* (Adventures in Japan) was published, not one of his best; it was credited as being done in collaboration with Otto, but considering the present condition of the Max Brod Archives, it is difficult to discover what Otto actually contributed. More important, Max Brod, in his autobiographical volume *Der Prager Kreis*, 1966 (The Prague Circle), gives a full account of Otto's later, unfortunately unfinished historical novel about the Calas affair, concerning Voltaire's efforts to clear the memory of the Protestant merchant Jean Calas, accused of killing his son who wanted to convert to Catholicism, and to assure justice for his wife and children. Max Brod himself confessed that he tried to complete the novel but could not succeed because he felt that Voltaire, taken all in all, was a rather dubious character.

Max Brod left Prague on the last train to Poland before the Wehrmacht occupied his hometown, and Otto and his family were deported on 10 December 1942 to Theresienstadt, a small town that was gradually evacuated to serve as a prison and a transition camp for Czech and European Jews being transported to the death camps in the east. Nearly a thousand prisoners were busy in its various offices, running a Kafkaesque internal administration, and Otto Brod was appointed by the Jewish Council of Elders to be senior clerk (*Sachbearbeiter*) for the distribution of printed forms, inevitably used by the bureaucracy of victims. He also took part in theatrical performances and lectures, presented in Theresienstadt's attics and cellars, speaking about "the Jewish image of the world" and, in a philosophical series in which Chief Rabbi Leo Baeck participated, about the question of free will; his brother, in Israel, would have been immensely happy to know that Otto also lectured on the achievements of Max Brod. Otto Brod and his wife, Tereza, were deported to the east in one of the last transports from Theresienstadt on 28 October 1944 and were immediately killed in the gas chambers upon arrival at Auschwitz. Their daughter Marianne, who had appeared in a well-remembered Theresienstadt performance of Verdi's *Requiem*, had been separated from her parents; she was transported to Bergen-Belsen (where Kafka's Milena had died) and was murdered there not much later.

Max Brod may have expected that his brother would return from Theresienstadt after the war. In his poem "Hotel in Haifa, 1943," he reveals that he was fully aware of the terrible conditions of the prison camp, though he did not know about the transports to the east yet. He writes of his own comfortable hotel room, almost European in appearance, and of wanting to be alone to continue studying Kant and the medieval religious philosopher Cusanus—but he buys himself a newspaper in the street, reads about the brutality of the war, and cannot avoid imagining the camp in which his brother, though he did not commit any crime, slowly dies of hunger: *Theresienstadt*, a word, a nightmare, a curse, that threatens to destroy the meaning of the world. In a later poem *Dem Bruder* (To My Brother), Max Brod offers a dirge to his brother's memory, heartrending because it is so simple in its words and wishes. He recalls his radiant presence in years gone by and thinks of the emptiness of the future; he had hoped to welcome Otto in Israel and to walk with him through his new homeland, laughing at the little donkeys, admiring the bazaars of Jaffa, visiting the town of Ramallah and the village of Gezer, thinking of King Solomon, standing on the blessed hills of Jerusalem, *"Orangen im gründunklen Blättersaal,"* oranges in the dark green hall of leaves. It is as if Otto's terrible death darkened "the roads and the land and the towns and the hills" and extinguished the light that the brothers had carried in their *one* heart.

CHAPTER ELEVEN

D'Annunzio: Poet and Aviator

D'ANNUNZIO was not a writer to keep art and life separate. In his middle years (1897–1909), when he resided at his magnificent Villa Capponcina, near Florence, his lifestyle (as long as he found willing creditors) was that of the grand *seigneur* of old times who surrounded himself with twenty cooks, maids, valets, gardeners, and stable boys. His secretary Tom Antongini lists the names of thirty-six pet dogs and thirty-one horses, not to mention about two hundred pigeons and five cats. A wonderfully erudite writer and an indefatigable student of the ancients, d'Annunzio was for a long time indifferent to modern technology. His military service was rather unheroic, first long postponed and later shortened by convenient furloughs—yet, as early as 1888, he wrote a series of patriotic articles declaring his enthusiasm for the Italian navy, which powerfully shielded Venice and the Adriatic coast, and celebrated the nation's naval heritage, "none more deeply national" and "perpetuated from century to century in the spirit of the Italian people."

The navy was, among the branches of Italian military power, his first love, and when war came to Italy in 1915, d'Annunzio attacked Austro-Hungarian ports on the Dalmatian coast. (The authorities allowed him to call himself *Il Commandante* and to undertake private war exploits, to the applause of the media.) I only regret that the Austrian poet Hugo von Hofmannsthal, instead of working in the Vienna War Archive, did not enlist in the Austrian navy to defend the imperial coastline against his cherished ally on the aesthetic front. Later in d'Annunzio's life, the swift boat in which he had attacked the Austrian defenses of Buccari in a much-celebrated but totally ineffective surprise assault (February 1918) found shelter in his villa, Il Vittoriale, and the thankful Italian navy donated to him the prow of the ship *Puglia*, which he put up, tower, deck, and cannons, in his park. It is still visited today by schoolchildren and international tourists.

But d'Annunzio was not the man to be true to his first love, or to his second or third, for that matter, and in his middle years he was introduced to the world of fast cars and the new achievements of the flying machines. The woman who showed him the way to automobiles and airplanes was Countess Giuseppina Mancini. Unfortunately, as time went on and the skepticism of d'Annunzio's biographers intensified, she had mixed reviews, if not a bad press. In early books about the poet's life, she was still an elegant woman of the Florentine aristocracy, attractive, not really slim but statuesque. She suffered in an awful childless marriage with a *brutalissimo* husband who was interested more in his vineyards and other women than in her. It should be added

that Count Mancini, who wrote poetry himself, invited d'Annunzio to his villa, for the poet willingly praised his products,
and he turned grimly jealous only when he received a few anonymous letters informing him of his wife's romantic disloyalty. In
Paolo Alatri's and John Woodhouse's more sober accounts of
d'Annunzio's life and work, Giuseppina Mancini has become a
petite bourgeoise from the Romagna of plump body, religious
anxieties, and lack of education, pushed by her conservative father—yet the letters published posthumously show her as a
woman capable of true passion, trying to return the poet to the
light of inherited Christianity, and ready to allude to Isolde and
Tristan in search of endless nights of ecstasy. D'Annunzio told
his publisher, in his own cool way, that he lived with her *priapicamente*, and put her in his next novel.

To say, as do many of the poet's biographers, that the Countess Mancini, lacking background and education, could not, and
did not, inspire him to write anything of importance, is to reduce d'Annunzio's way of writing to the old commonplace of
the Muse and the writer who depends on her transcendental
dictation. D'Annunzio wrote in a different, almost vampirelike,
way; he sucked the blood and feelings of his women, and if those
women did not suffer enough (often clinically or in hospitals),
he psychologically tortured them, even Eleonora Duse, and imbibed the effluvia of their bitter humiliations. A feminist biography of d'Annunzio has not been written yet. He deftly
managed his overlapping affairs: Alexandra di Rudini and
Countess Mancini at the beginning of 1907, and the latter along
with a Russian countess toward the end of 1908. His manuscript

Solus ad solam (A Man Alone to a Woman Alone), published posthumously in 1939, purports to be a long account of Mancini's insanity, triggered by his break with her, but d'Annunzio cannot easily give up his games and he includes a few pages, surprisingly self-ironic, about how he tried to persuade his Czech translator, Marie Votruba (Votrubová), to share his bed (there are appropriate lines about the hills of Prague and the Austrian tyranny over the Czechs). She played along for a while, enjoying the situation in her down-to-earth way, but refused to be caught in his clutches. Proceeding as he usually did, he used medical reports about the insanity of the countess in the final chapter of his novel *Forse che sì, forse che no* (often transferring entire paragraphs from *Solus ad solam*), leaving the deranged woman in a closed institution where she is held for three years.

Caught in her unhappy marriage, Countess Mancini had restlessly established her own interests, bought a new car, and eagerly cultivated the nascent fashion of the flying machines. It was she who brought d'Annunzio to Brescia to attend the international car races of 1907, and we soon hear that the poet acquired a car of his own, an aggressively red Fiorentina speedster (registration number 21-445) which he called *Per Non Dormire*, an imperative that often adorned his letter paper. In his roadster he dashed around the Tuscan countryside (as do Paolo Tarsis and Isabella in the first chapter of the novel), much to the ire of the peasants and police. On 24 June 1909, two village carabinieri ticketed him for speeding, to use the American idiom, rather than the language of Italian bureaucracy, "for driving at a velocity superior to that normally permitted" (article 67 of the traf-

Countess Giuseppina Mancini.

fic regulations confirmed by royal decree of 8 January 1905). The poet was asked to appear in court at Siena, and his traffic violation was widely reported in the Italian and the French press, including the *Journal des Débats*.

"It is well known," one newspaper disclosed, "that the famous sportmann [*sic*] d'Annunzio, now so much interested in flying, has not given up riding and driving his automobile," and the poet was quoted saying that his name would not be d'Annunzio if he had not tried to surpass "normal" speed. Acting in due process, the bureaucracy began to investigate the sinner's previous record, and it turned out that he was once fined twenty lire for dueling, and twice, on 29 October and in December 1908, for speeding. The trial was to be held on 23 November 1909, a Siena judge presiding, just before which the poet sent a politely condescending telegram explaining that he could not attend personally but had entrusted his case to the able hands of his attorney. An adjournment was declared, and by 1910 d'Annunzio had removed himself to France to escape his creditors.

If it is true (as John Woodhouse suggests) that d'Annunzio had accompanied the countess to early flight demonstrations, they could have been only those by the French aviator Léon Delagrange, who came to Rome in late May 1908, to Milan in June, and Turin in early July. They were not really awe-inspiring, and if d'Annunzio was there, his *Notebooks* do not say anything about them. Yet d'Annunzio was keen on flying by that time, and was possibly toying with the idea of a cutting-edge novel about flying. A group of Roman enthusiasts had succeeded in gathering enough money (with a little help from the war ministry) to invite Wilbur Wright, who wanted to sell his planes, to the Roman field of Centocelle; and in the spring of 1909 an Italian aviation "school" was established there. That is, Wilbur Wright took up a few influential people in the air and gave a few hours of instruction to Lieutenant Mario Calderara, who had flown earlier from French airfields. Calderara was then declared fully qualified to pass his skills on to his friend Lieutenant Umberto Savoia, of the Italian Pioneer Corps. D'Annunzio, who was there, closely observed what was going on and tried to absorb the technical parlance of the mechanics and pilots. As two letters published only recently indicate, he was on friendly terms with Calderara, whom he admired as much as he admired other people knowledgeable about plane construction and flying. His *Notebooks* reveal little, but he neatly entered Calderara's street address, Roma, via del Corso, 52.

On 10 September, d'Annunzio arrived at Brescia (from a villa at Marina di Pisa) to attend the events on the airfield for three days. He had been working assiduously on his "aviation" novel for a month or so, and his mind was set to watch the action at close range, to listen to the jargon of the professionals, to jot down useful observations in his *Notebooks* as if he were a disciple of Zola, and, most important, to go up with one of the pilots for a first flight of his own. He walked around the hangars as eagerly as Franz Kafka would later, and noted, for future reference, the less than noble details: the mechanics' folded beds, their coarse boots dirtied by the *brughiera* soil, their sweaty shirts, iron wires hanging from a nail on a wall, or that grotesque mechanic hopping around on a goat (he reappears in the novel). A few notes described how a pilot, or a mechanic, fills the gas tank, first measuring what he needs with a dipstick and then pouring gasoline through a yellow cloth filter from a canister painted white. Yet, in spite of his declared interest in technical procedures and objects, motors, steel cords, wood, oilcloth and

all, at least half of his notes turn to views of the *brughiera* landscape, the hills and distant mountains. He feels aesthetic pleasure in taking down the names of places and mountains, the
façade of the Montichiari Cathedral, the church of Castiglione,
the marvelous "curtain" of poplar trees separating the district
of Ghedi from that of Montichiari, the clouds above Monte
Baldo, and the eternal chirping of the swallows (a leitmotif in
the novel). A true impressionist, he is enchanted by the changing light of day, observes the brilliance of distant farms and
nearby fences in the sun, the approaching shadows of the evening here and there, and even adds a little pencil sketch showing
how the struts and braces of an airplane, *la nervatura delle ali*,
form a distinct pattern of squares when seen against the sun. He
simply cannot resist aestheticizing technical matter.

Watching and listening to the pilots and mechanics at Centocelle and at the Brescia aerodrome, the poet d'Annunzio was
concerned with the Franglais of the professionals, and since he
was (like R. M. Rilke) an avid reader of old dictionaries, he was
constantly searching for Italian equivalents for what the new
aviators called *gauchissement* or *mise au point*. He complained about
the linguistic problems to Barzini, who observed that d'Annunzio was eager to reinvent appropriate terms by taking them,
if at all possible, from the ancient vocabulary of seamen and
sailors—terms that, as d'Annunzio said, were "full of expressiv-
ity and sounds, and a strange reawakening of images"; even
though they were forgotten or ignored, they concealed a "potential power of description coming alive in denoting new things."
If d'Annunzio said in an interview that he had devised two

thousand technical terms when writing his aviation novel, he was exaggerating, as usual, but it is true that he tried, unfortunately with little success, to recommend the old Venetian navy terms *fusoliera* for "fuselage" and *velivolo* for "airplane." Many commentators, especially outside Italy, believe that *velivolo* was a poetic term entirely of the poet's invention, but it may be found in the dictionaries of Algarotti (1764) and even Florio (1598), meaning any conveyance that moves as if carried by full sails. The Latin *velivolu(m)* denoted the sea plowed by ships, an image particularly dear to d'Annunzio and derived from Vergil or Ovid. "It is a light word," he said in an interview in November 1909, a few weeks after Brescia, "fluid, of rapid motion, and does not impede the tongue or contract the mouth. It is easily pronounced, bears a certain phonetic resemblance to the familiar *veicolo*, and can be used by the educated and the uneducated alike. It is of ancient origin and yet expresses, with admirable propriety, the essence and the motion of the most modern machines." It was d'Annunzio's secret that he had used the word, in the ancient meaning, in his first collection of verse, *Primo vere* (1879), written when he was sixteen years old.

The story of d'Annunzio's first flight(s) in a *velivolo* has long turned into legend for many reasons, and it is a pity that the film of it, made by an unknown cameraman on that occasion, was lost. We have the reports of the untiring local reporters and, above all, Barzini's account in *Corriere della Sera*; and since Barzini wanted to fly himself, he looked closely at what his colleague, the national bard, was up to. When d'Annunzio arrived, he wanted to fly with Blériot, at that moment the most famous aviator of them all. In a telegram, his usual way of communication, to Countess Goloubeff, who had succeeded Giuseppina Mancini, d'Annunzio said so openly and added in a letter of 11 September 1909 that he liked Blériot a good deal (a simple and modest man, with a sweet air) and felt particularly charmed by the shape of his plane because it resembled the Egyptian image of the sacred ibis.

Blériot and Madame Blériot ("an overweight Juno" of vast bosom and excellent teeth, according to the poet) welcomed d'Annunzio personally, but to fly with him was another matter entirely. D'Annunzio mentioned in another communication to the countess, as if in passing, that flights with passengers had been postponed to the end of the races, when he would be gone from Brescia (not true, obviously). D'Annunzio, accompanied by Barzini, immediately paid homage to Blériot in his hangar, telling Barzini on the way that Blériot's personal account of crossing the Channel (later quoted verbatim in d'Annunzio's novel) reminded him of his own elegy on Icarus (especially the image of the sea, the ships down below, and the feeling of loneliness in space). At the hangar, d'Annunzio continued to quote his Icarus to Blériot, although the aviator did not respond at all to the noble thoughts and talked about other matters. No invitation to fly was forthcoming, but d'Annunzio did not cease to take notes about Blériot to be used in *Forse che sì, forse che no*.

When d'Annunzio visited Curtiss's hangar (where he encountered two American mechanics sitting on two little stools, puffing two little pipes), a mutual friend suggested to the American aviator that the Italian writer would like to join him for a flight.

Curtiss hesitated awhile, revealing that Luigi Barzini had expressed the same wish earlier (he had turned him down because he was too heavy), and ultimately relented. A famous photo was shot on that occasion; Curtiss with his best who-is-this-guy expression on his poker face, and d'Annunzio in his maroon jacket and gray gloves, with an uncertain smile like "a young monk" (as one of the local journalists wrote), or rather like a student on a school excursion.

As the plane began to move, all eyes were on d'Annunzio, but

Curtiss and d'Annunzio.

people could see only his legs because, as Barzini wrote, "the tyrannical laws of equilibrium" did not necessarily harmonize with the aviator's "hospitality." The plane wobbled its way on the uneven terrain, lifting and dropping its tail, rose for a few moments (*un instante di alcuni palmi*) and abruptly descended again, proceeding with an "earthy and modest gallop" until it came to a halt in the distance. D'Annunzio jumped out and tore his elegant clothes on some steel wire. I do not believe that Curtiss was ever serious about taking d'Annunzio up in his plane, and the poet put a brave face on a dubious if not comic situation, responding to questions about his brief flying experience with gusts of enthusiasm, as if intoxicated (Barzini noted) by the drop of a magic potion. "Flying is divine," d'Annunzio told the press, "divine and yet inexpressible." He was satisfied with little, evidently, and he continued to speak about his fleeting experience as an unforgettable moment of supreme joy, like one of those rare flashes of supreme happiness created by "luminous thrusts of life." (In his novel, the sexual connotations are far more audible.)

It was late, about 6:30 P.M. (12 September 1909), and officials and many people were leaving the field to get into their cars or find transport (in the ensuing jams, it took an hour to drive the twelve kilometers to Brescia). Fortunately, somebody in the crowd gathering around the poet mentioned that Calderara had not yet returned to the hangar, and d'Annunzio, recalling the days of Centocelle, immediately asked where he might be found. He was standing near the signal tower, and when he heard of d'Annunzio's wishes, he was happy to oblige. Calderara had just completed a flight with Savoia at his side, having turned a wide curve of three kilometers and then continuing with five more curves, softly landing; d'Annunzio could rely on his skills. It was a flight without any technical problems. The weights dropped from the catapult, and Calderara's Wright plane ran along the wooden rails, effortlessly rose in the air, and circled close to the grandstand in the "half-light of the evening." The patriots cheered the unique event bringing together the young pilot and inventor with the great poet of the "Latini" in an American machine fitted with an Italian Rebus motor. Immediately after landing, Barzini interviewed d'Annunzio (whom he called "an instrument of psychological precision on board a plane"). Considering the writings and soldierly deeds of the future aviator, it is striking that in his interview he combined self-analysis with an honest enthusiasm, with no anticipations of his patriotic belligerence later. He spoke only about his own personal experience and the sensations of his body, almost physiologically.

Earlier d'Annunzio had complained about the "defects" of planes, that is, the mind-stunning noise of the motor when starting and landing, but now he was ready to declare that the motor noise was "lively, sweet, and impulsive"; he said he was not even aware of the noise of Calderara's plane when it rose against the wind. In the immensity of space, he mused, all motor noise was lost; instead of stupefying the senses, it rather prompted them to concentrate and thus in itself became an element of pleasure. All the sensations are new—even the first moment of that empty feeling when the plane ascends turns into something desirable, a singular joy reminiscent of what people

feel on roller coasters, and in being aware of utter weightless-
ness, all burdens of matter left behind. We feel light, ephemeral,
transfigured! D'Annunzio enjoyed "the dreamlike change of
things seen from above"; he noticed horses on the ground gal-
loping as if they were hurried by wings, and yet in the change of
perspective they appeared fastened to the ground. "I wish I
could go up hundreds of meters in space! It would be an incom-
parable intoxication! Oh, I would give everything, everything, to
devote myself to flying!" He was in a triumphant mood, and
suggested banteringly to Calderara that they exchange professions: the pilot would write d'Annunzio's novels, and he, d'Annunzio, would fly. Calderara, quick at repartee and looking to
the future, responded that it was fully in the powers of the poet
to write and to fly as well. Six days later, while d'Annunzio was
inspecting the restoration of the mayor's palace at Bologna,
he gave an interview to a local newspaperman (18 September
1909), in which he reminisced about the glorious and indelible
experience of flying, and declared that he was to buy a plane
promptly to dedicate himself to flying. He did not say whether
he had the money for a flying machine, and his impatient creditors must have read his interview with cynical smiles.

IT IS INSUFFICIENT to deal with d'Annunzio's novel *Forse che
sì, forse che no* from a positivist perspective alone, saying that it
mirrors his interest in aviation or that he portrays Giuseppina
Mancini in the image of Isabella, or Mario Calderara in the character of Paolo Tarsis (Calderara deserves better). By its struc-

ture of metaphorical language and its arrangement of events, the novel closes itself off against fugitive experience while keeping it paradoxically alive so that it long survives the moment of inception and, whether the author wants it or not, is carried along in the minds of readers and interpreters. *Forse che sì, forse che no* has attracted far less attention than d'Annunzio's famous earlier novels; to this day there does not exist an English version, though the novel was immediately translated into French and, brilliantly, into German (1910) by none other than Carl Vollmöller, who happened to be a gifted writer close to the Expressionists and the coauthor of the screenplay for Marlene Dietrich's *Blue Angel* film. I suspect that the translator Georgina Harding, who had dealt with d'Annunzio's earlier novels in the Victorian way in which Constance Garnett handled Dostoyevski, (censoring what she thought to be the immoral passages), would not have touched *Forse che sì, forse che no* with a ten-foot pole. In an interview in *La Tribuna* (January 1910), d'Annunzio himself tried to suggest that the aviation parts of the story were less central than the drama of excited passions (an understatement, considering the sadomasochism, incest, and suicide in the novel), and it is true, at least at first sight, that the aviation sequences are simply a kind of frame at the beginning and end of the story. However, a closer reading reveals that the flight sequences reappear in the core of the intimate stories, not to speak of the images of flying that punctuate the entire text.

To fly means, in d'Annunzio's novel, to transform a technical feat into a heroic action of supreme and pure energy, enabling the aviator to soar high above everything terrestrial and profane, all the dismal snares that are the fate of man. In the beginning of the story, Guido Cambiasi, who breaks an altitude record only to crash and die, sets the emblematic norm while he rises far above the crowds and the other pilots who just want to satisfy their vanity or grab the awards. His close friend Paolo Tarsis follows his (and Blériot's) famous example, flies from the Italian mainland over the sea to Sardinia, a feat never attempted before, makes a victorious and lonely landing there, and cools his wounded foot, hurt in the landing, in the consoling waves of the ocean: "since he was completely exhausted and could not bear his pain walking, he slowly dragged himself toward the water and dipped his feet into the sea." The aviator-superman deeply distrusts women; young Vana, in the early stirrings of her emotions, first believes she loves Cambiasi, but, after he dies, transfers her intense feelings to Paolo and finds herself in competition with her older sister (a fin de siècle dominatrix) Isabella Inghirami, who luxuriates in Paolo's embraces. Isabella taunts and tortures Paolo to inflame his passions and to make him dependent on her, giving and willfully withholding herself from him, *forse che sì, forse che no*. When Vana, suddenly hating her sister, wants to separate the lovers and win Paolo for herself, she tells him of an incestuous relationship between Isabella and their brother Aldo. Isabella, far too proud to defend herself, uses Vana's accusation to challenge Paolo— "we all should be pensive brothers in lust"—and goes mad after Paolo has almost killed her in a last embrace, or rather rape. Vana kills herself with an ancient dagger, seeing that she has been unable to attract Paolo to herself. Aldo may cut a *bella figura*, but he certainly does not convince anybody as an incestuous brother. I suspect that the idea of incest burns, for the most part, as an imaginary fire in the minds of the sisters—the younger woman uses the idea as a weapon to destroy, and her older sister exploits it as an instrument to humiliate her lover. This is misogyny without a palliative counterargument; when Paolo ultimately escapes into the clouds, he leaves behind Vana, dead, and Isabella, insane.

Forse che sì, forse che no can be read, whether it is an aviation story or not, as an exasperating and baroque novel of rare strength and lyrical splendor, combining the most sentimental kitsch with passages of almost blinding poetry. It may be to its advantage that it screens its exaggerated characters, always hovering *sur l'abîme* (of volcanic precipices, or in bed and in the skies), half-hidden behind entire chains of metaphors and Homeric similes, both trite and of barbarous energy. True, d'Annunzio's show-off erudition borders on the absurd ("Do you remember Beethoven's twentieth variation on a Diabelli theme dedicated to Antonie Brentano?"), his descriptions of the moldering walls of Mantua castle are too archaeological to sustain interest, and Isabella's recurrent striptease performances, revealing her impeccable corsets, garters, and stockings, pander to an old-fashioned *frisson*. (The situation has been grasped recently by a California porn producer who proudly calls himself Paolo Tarsis.) The list of the novel's failures may be long, but it is balanced, I believe, by the Balzacian *furioso* of its dramatic scenes (within a theater of the mind), the effective leitmotif technique, close to that of Thomas Mann (alas, d'Annunzio has a particular fixation about the play of ladies' knees under long skirts and the blond hair of their armpits seen when they pull up their sleeves), and his art of the objective correlative—for example, the ugly and inimical whirling of bats in an old tomb suggesting something of the secret chaos in the minds of Aldo and Vana. D'Annunzio again and again shows the full power of his lyrical rather than narrative art when writing of changing cloud formations, a favorite topos of his. Many landscape images are precise and inimitable: "the entire landscape resounded as if every hill were a kettledrum turned upside down" ("*tutta la . . . campagna . . . era sonora come se ogni monticello fosse un timpano rovescio*").

Even when d'Annunzio transfers entire paragraphs from his *Notebooks* to his novel, they function differently in the fiction context, and his Brescia aerodrome differs radically from that of the local journalists, and from the reports of Kafka and Brod, for that matter. His *passéisme* (to use a Futurist term for denigrating the traditionalists) looks back into history; and while even the Futurists would have liked his comparison of the air show as a "gathering of war" (*dieta di guerra*), his descriptive vocabulary takes on an antique and heroic tinge when he writes that the air-field looks "like an arsenal" or "citadel." The rough hangars, which Max Brod compared to the clubhouses of rowing clubs and in the ultimate implications of Kafka's text resemble grand *pissoirs*, to d'Annunzio appear to be shipyards where, in ancient times, galleys were repaired and outfitted. The system of flags and pennants, of technical relevance to the races, changes into a celebratory "parade of banners," and the painted signs on the fronts of the hangars remind him of the pennons of military contingents of the old Italian city-states. In a bold stroke, his *passéisme* deepens into mythology; he places on the modern airfield a famous bronze statue, the Victoria of the temple of the emperor Flavius Vespasianus, because he needs, in the midst of all the imperfections, an "image of beauty" and "perfection"—admittedly, much to the displeasure of the pilots, who regard the statue (transported to the airfield on a simple peasant cart drawn by six Lombard oxen) as an impediment. Yet the statue is of high symbolic value because on its plinths the new statue of Guido Cambiasi will be placed to remind the masses of his lonely heroism. D'Annunzio had visited the Brescia city museum, where he had admired the statue, as his *Notebooks* suggest, but the possibility cannot be excluded that d'Annunzio took his idea from Aldo Mazza's official poster of the air races, showing a Victoria of ancient mythology next to a Wright plane that nearly touches her fluttering chiton and a little zeppelin in the background among the clouds.

Blériot may have disappointed d'Annunzio by not inviting him to fly, but he remained, to the novelist, a towering figure of stubborn triumph over the elements, and he is present throughout the novel, though the writer does not mention his name, relying on easy recognition by the reader. In one of d'Annunzio's breathless descriptions of air traffic (as if all planes started and landed concurrently), he writes of crashes, mishaps, and hurt pilots. In a particularly vivid scene, he watches a plane suddenly burning in the air, "seized by a fire without color," abruptly going down as the flames begin to destroy the entire structure; the

pilot, his clothes on fire, jumps out and rolls on the grass trying
to extinguish the flames with his bare hands. He stands there
"black, sooty, dirty with oil, his hair singed"—the exact image
of Blériot's mishap, and of the burned plane, during the aviation
week at Rheims, transferred by d'Annunzio to Brescia. (He
strangely antedates the Brescia events, transferring them to the
earlier Rheims week in late August, which he did not attend.)
Felix Philipp Ingold has pointed out that Blériot is even more
literally present when Paolo Tarsis, caught in Isabella's embrace
and toying with her breasts, suddenly imagines himself in full
flight, sees his plane high in the sky, and remembers Blériot's pilot's cap, his sharp Gallic profile, the strong chin, the marked
cheekbones, and a whorl of hair on his forehead (exactly as they
appear in d'Annunzio's *Notebooks*). In his wish to identify with
Blériot at this moment of sexual captivity, Paolo "dreams," as it
were, of Blériot's historic crossing of the Channel and the "brief
story of the hero" resounds in his consciousness—"like the
rapid thrust of a wind in a ship's rigging." The text shifts, after
a discreet quotation mark, to a nearly thirty-line excerpt from
Blériot's own narrative as published in the international newspapers. Blériot has inspired Paolo to cross the sea from Italy to
Sardinia, and Ingold is certainly right to say that d'Annunzio's
passages about Paolo's state of mind when crossing the sea can
be read as a "paraphrase" of Blériot's narrative. I would even say
that it subtly fuses reminiscences of Blériot, d'Annunzio's allusion to his Icarus poem, and Paolo's thoughts in an inventive
monologue intérieur indirect in which the narrator artfully combines
a wealth of textual materials.

The entire air show at Brescia is seen, in the novel, through the eyes of the supermen Cambiasi and Tarsis, who look down on the field, and the world, even when they are not in the air. They have been training together and their lives have run a parallel course; they have served first on an Italian battleship and then a submarine, a particularly harsh experience. Later they decide that a discipline merely imposed from above is not sufficient and they travel around the world, braving impossible adventures in China, Outer Mongolia, Africa (the narrative often reads like a parody of Luigi Barzini's popular travelogues), until they construct their own planes and triumph as aviators. They condescend to notice other pilots, these "mercurial mercenaries" in the service of an industry that pays for their feats, and they laugh at foolish inventors with their monstrous machines, *ornithoptères*, or planes with twenty wings stacked one above the other, hopelessly immobile and never leaving the ground. Paolo looks at the hangars and finds there, perhaps not without reason, "the tragic and the ridiculous," side by side. It is dubious enough that some pilots gather their families in the hangars, "honest housewives, healthy children, even wet nurses and tutors." Worse still, there are women groupies who hang around the aviators and their machines, "smooth, perfumed, and wanton," and, like Isabella, "quick morays," totally "perverse and unfathomable." The "eagle" Paolo, following his friend, soars above "the chicken," an anarchist and aristocrat (his understanding of Nietzsche), and celebrates a victory that smacks of the inhuman. The narrator suggests that people on the ground feel "renewed" by his infinite energy, and while it may be difficult to conclude that a new cult of a *Führer*, fascist or otherwise, constitutes the heart of the matter, it is not far away.

THE AVIATION NOVEL sold well, and d'Annunzio was asked whether he wanted to give public lectures about the history and future of the new flying machines. He agreed to do so, if only for urgent financial reasons. Pilade Frattini, the imaginative manager of his lectures, sent him to a dozen cities in northern Italy, where the biggest theaters were rented to accommodate the largest audiences, and d'Annunzio was to speak on "Domination of the Skies." He introduced each lecture by celebrating the city in which he was addressing his audience—Milan, Turin, Venice, Vincenza, Bergamo, and Verona—and in the core of his discourse he radically revised his history of flying from how he had presented it in his novel. There it had been a matter of sending the Italians to the Nietzschean school of flying to educate them in pride and heroism. Here, in the public lecture a year later, he was concerned more with Italy in the context of international politics, and shifted his full attention to France, the "great *maestra* of aviation." It is not a mere coincidence that the lectures for Trieste and Trento were forbidden by the Austrian police, who suspected d'Annunzio of irredentist propaganda, and rightly so. (At the Teatro Lirico in Milan, the gallery had been quick to shout *"Abasso l'Austria!"* [Down with Austria!].) France emerged, in these lectures, as the grand and worthy ally of Italy in the conflicts of the future, and instead of linking Leonardo da Vinci to Lilienthal and the brothers Wright, d'Annunzio interpreted da Vinci as a forerunner of the engineer Clément Ader, a great and tragic figure in French aviation. In the novel, Ader is not mentioned at all, but in the lectures d'Annunzio took great care to speak about the construction of his planes and his experiments (1890–97), and he also included the names of other French pilots such as Paulhan and Rougier (the hero of Brescia). Unfortunately, d'Annunzio did not want to go on lecturing for too long, and when ticket sales in Verona dropped, he immediately quit the enterprise.

By March 1910, d'Annunzio's financial situation had become untenable, and to avoid his creditors and legal proceedings, he exiled himself to Paris and later to Arcachon, on the Atlantic shore of France, where he tried to resuscitate (together with the Russian countess) the seigneurial glories of his lost Capponcina, at least on a minor scale. Claude Debussy wrote the music to one of his plays performed at a Paris theater, and he had to concentrate on writing, not flying, as he had hoped. Consequently, when, in October 1911, Italy, continuing its colonial adventures, invaded Tripoli, then under Turkish hegemony, d'Annunzio missed his chance to watch at close range how the nascent Italian air force strafed and bombed Arab positions. It was Captain Carlo Maria Piazza who did so (the first in history), and F. T. Marinetti, chief of the Futurists, rewrote Piazza's report to the *Corriere della Sera* (20 November 1911). His staccato experimental text is composed strictly according to Futurist theory (mostly nouns and verbs in the infinitive), as argued in his *Supplement to the Technical Manifesto of Futurist Literature* (11 August 1912). In matters of military exploits, patriotism, and airplanes,

Marinetti and d'Annunzio were competitors, rather than allies, and while the Tripoli round undoubtedly went to Marinetti, d'Annunzio applied himself to technological modernity in his own way, perhaps with more lasting import than Marinetti's Piazza piece. He began working with the early Turin film industry and importantly contributed to Giovanni Pastrone's production of *Cabiria*, an exemplary blood-and-sandals epic at the origin of the genre, inventing, among others, the mighty figure of Maciste. This version of Batman was purely pectoral and survived, in Italian films and on television, at least two generations, if not more.

In the spring of 1915 (after his financial situation had been stabilized by his loyal publisher, the owner of *Corriere della Sera*, and other friends), d'Annunzio was more than eager to return from exile to push for Italy's entry into the war on the side of the Entente. He came back to his homeland on 3 May, but he did not yet know that Italy had signed, on 26 April, the secret Treaty of London with the Entente against the imperial monarchy of Austria-Hungary, and he had to pretend later when he made his war speeches (often anticipating Mussolini's rhetoric) that he had known of the negotiations between Rome and London that resulted, in due course, in a change of government. Antonio Salandra became prime minister and a general mobilization was called on 24 May 1915 against Austria.

At fifty-two years old, d'Annunzio was granted his request to be recommissioned as lieutenant of the Novara Lancers, attached to the headquarters of the Third Army under the command of the Duke d'Aosta, and permitted "to participate in any military operation along the entire line held by the armed forces." He took lodgings at the Venice Hotel Royal-Danieli, and later rented Fritz von Hohenlohe's Casetta Rossa on the Grand Canal, whose noble landlord, of Italian sympathies but residing in Switzerland, guaranteed the services of a cook, a *cameriera* (active in the bedroom), two valets, and the appropriate *gondoliere*. He had great plans, tremendously enjoyed his new uniform, and chased Austrian ships on board the torpedo boat *Intrepid*. The military authorities soon recognized that they had a problem, *un guaio*, on their hands. D'Annunzio had to mobilize his best rhetoric to convince the generals in a plea for permission to undertake a flight over Trieste. After some hesitations (considering his international fame), a flight test was arranged, and on 7 August 1915 he was piloted by Giovanni Miraglia (who was to die shortly thereafter in a crash) over Trieste. Leaflets were dispersed over the city, saying that twenty thousand Austrians had recently been taken prisoner and that the Italian flag would be planted victoriously on San Giusto hill. A member of the Italian government remarked dryly that d'Annunzio's text oscillated between puerile ranting and the prophecies of Superman, and it was not the last time.

The Austrian high command, it was said, put a prize of twenty thousand crowns on d'Annunzio's head, and people speculated that the Austrians bombed Venice only to hit the Casetta Rossa, but, needless to say, their bombs fell on the palazzo exactly opposite across the Grand Canal where the poet's aristocratic mistress lived (one of them, and she was not at home).

D'Annunzio was restless; in early August he joined the crew

of a submarine on its hundredth mission against the enemy (the promised submarine novel remained unwritten), and about a month later he was in the air again, flying over Trento to disperse leaflets addressing the Trentini as people of love and suffering and eruditely comparing the airplanes to "the bronze dagger of Dante," raised in their defense. On 16 June 1916, he was again flying over Trieste, but the Austrians were better prepared to welcome the poet, the antiaircraft fire was murderous, his pilot, Luigi Bologna, had to make an emergency landing on the sea near Grado, and d'Annunzio hit his head on the muzzle of the machine gun, gravely wounding his right eye and temple. In his soldier's pride, he pretended that nothing had happened, flew another mission over Trieste next day, missed an unfortunate raid against Ljubljana, and was declared almost blind when he finally turned to the medics. He was told absolutely not to move, but he had himself carried to Venice, where his daughter (meanwhile married to an air force officer) patiently supervised his long convalescence and provided him, possibly against the wishes of the ophthalmologist, with strips of paper and a pencil to write in bed.

His *Notturno*, published only in the early 1920s, as if in a dream of blindness and suffering and yet a "divine truce" (*divina tregua*), liberated itself, word by word and hesitant sentence after sentence, from traditional rhetoric, and it holds out an undaunted lyricism. He thinks of a fellow pilot, now buried; the house of his childhood at Pescara; Venice in the wintry fog; his mother's love; the first steps into a fragrant garden—moments of a glowing and forthright self-exploration rarely to be found in any of his books again.

The aviator d'Annunzio not only wrote a lyrical *Notturno* or, while flying over enemy territory, staccato notes passed back and forth between observer and pilot (the absolute realization of Marinetti's theory of the Futurist text), but was also the author of a memorandum "about the use of bomber squadrons in future operations," officially submitted on 17 May 1917 to Luigi Cadorna, commander in chief. Cadorna was well known, or rather infamous, for his use of frontal infantry attacks in alpine regions, regardless of human losses. Signing his memorandum "Captain Aviator," the poet offered headquarters a unique combination of imaginative foresight and technological knowledge (with the help of Gianni Caproni, builder of warplanes). He argued that the Italian air force had long passed its age of doubts and hesitations (though admittedly starting from scratch) and, in the future, should not any longer be considered an "auxiliary force" but an "essential branch" of the armed forces, operating, ultimately, to search for and destroy enemy industrial production sites while protecting the assembling of Italian war matériel.

Reading the document, one must consider the moment: the writers H. G. Wells, in England, and Rudolf Martin, in Germany, had described fictional bombing raids on major European and American cities even before the war broke out and London was attacked by German zeppelins. D'Annunzio was not writing fiction, but was practically telling the commander in chief what to do with his airplanes. It is too early to organize any "inter-allied" aerial undertaking, he suggests realistically, and recommends that any national air force do what it can achieve most effectively.

As a hypothetical and tempting example, he speaks of bombing Krupp's Essen; assuming that Italian triplanes, with their six-hundred-horsepower engines, were capable of flying eight hours with an average speed of 100–130 kph, they could easily carry a load of 1,200 kilograms of explosives. D'Annunzio wanted to whet the commander's appetite, I believe; once he has caught his attention, he develops a set of specific ideas for the use of squadrons actually available to attack Austrian bases in "Dalmatia Latina" to lessen the burden of the navy and to prepare the ground, by aerial bombardment, for subsequent infantry offensives. It was especially important to destroy enemy communications in the rear, particularly those between Bolzano and Franzensfeste, to prepare the liberation of the Trentino, that enslaved region (*la terra schiava*). Strange: a poet much gifted lyrically, and yet a coolheaded planner of destruction in the service of his country. Not even Ernst Jünger, who had deeper perceptions, is an appropriate analogy. It is no coincidence that Italian infantrymen, in mutiny against the slaughter, threatened to kill d'Annunzio, and he looked on dispassionately as thirty-eight of them were executed. At least he did show signs of emotion when he remembered these events in 1923, John Woodhouse reminds us.

On 13 September 1916, d'Annunzio, in spite of all the warnings of the physicians, was in the air again and felt reborn (*ero rinato*), as he wrote in the addenda to his *Notturno*. He flew together with an entire squadron, piloted by his friend "Gigi" Bologna, east against the base of Parenzo—as observer (who had just escaped blindness) and bombardier (who held a bomb cage between his legs and dropped all four of the bombs by hand). In the following year, after he had fought courageously with the infantry, he undertook new bombing raids against the Austrians. He braved the searchlights and massive antiaircraft fire over Pola (where James Joyce had taught English to the officers' corps before going to Trieste to work on his *Ulysses*), and raided Cattaro, the main submarine base, after long and possibly futile preparations because only two of fourteen planes were able to reach the scheduled target without getting lost over the sea.

But more was needed, and the poet, who had mentioned a flight over Vienna in his earlier lectures (1910), again thought of attacking the imperial city in 1915 and mentioned the (im)possibility of such a flight with mere three-hundred-horsepower engines in his *La Leda senza cigno*, 1916 (Leda Without a Swan). He made himself a nuisance at the high command by repeatedly presenting his arguments, and even prepared a leaflet speaking about "the senile city of the deluded last Habsburgian" (Emperor Charles), the clash between "Latin nobility" and "the brutality of the barbarians." He concluded this text, which was to be dropped on the unsuspecting population (perhaps he remembered his visits to Vienna in 1899 and 1900 with Eleonora Duse, when he admired the art collections and the incredibly blond women with astonishingly fat behinds), with a few remarks about people who were worthy of surviving if only to see the light of the approaching Italian victories—not a particularly effective argument in psychological warfare. The commander in chief gave d'Annunzio the polite runaround, and difficulties mounted. One officer was hurt in a mishap, another died in a crash, a test flight was demanded (which d'Annunzio passed with flying colors). Finally the high command relented and gave permission, saying that his flight was to be undertaken strictly

The projected flight plan of d'Annunzio's raid on Vienna.

for "political and demonstrative purposes," without threatening
the city in any way and avoiding dogfights with enemy aircraft.
The raid was to show, the order stated, "the uncontested
power" of Italian aircraft in Viennese airspace, as a "symbol of
the innate energy" of the Italian race (*razza*). All credit was
given to the poet as the leader and initiator of the raid, but the
military command of the squadron was nevertheless delegated
to a military professional.

After some confusing delays (partly because of bad weather
over the Alps), on 9 August 1918, at 5:15 in the morning, eleven
planes of the 87th Squadron and one biplane (carrying d'Annunzio and his pilot) finally rose to the skies from San Pelagio airfield near Padua in tight formation, to be kept throughout the
entire mission. Not all the planes were to reach Vienna. Almost
immediately after takeoff, Captain Alberto Masprone, the actual
commander of the flight, developed engine trouble and was
forced to land, nearly destroying his plane and hurting his jaw-
bone. Not much later, Francesco Ferrini and Vincenzo Contratti
had to return to camp because of the irregular performance of
their engines, leaving Natale Palli (the poet's pilot) in charge
and eight planes altogether to continue on their course of more
than a thousand kilometers. They crossed the Piave River, by-
passed Udine and Klagenfurt, and approached Vienna via the
Rax Mountains, Wiener Neustadt, and Baden.

By 8:15 A.M., at an altitude of two thousand meters, d'Annunzio, as usual, jotted down a few notes observing the progress
of the flight near the Alpine Teufelswand and the Wiener Neustadt airfield, where a group of six idle fighter planes was visi-

ble. He also noticed that one of his fellow pilots had to give up because of engine malfunction. (It was Giovanni Sarti, born in Barcelona, Spain, who made a safe landing near Schwarzau, on the Steinfeld near Wiener Neustadt, burned his plane, strictly according to orders, was promptly arrested, and, according to the protocol of his interrogation kept at the Vienna Kriegs-archiv, talked a good deal about the dubious SVA motor and his shattered nerves because of his incessant duties at the front.) By 9:10 A.M., at three thousand meters, d'Annunzio noted that the sun was coming up over the Wienerwald, and by 9:20 the seven had reached Vienna and opened their containers of leaflets over the central districts of the city, especially over the Graben and the cathedral of St. Stephen, while the citizens, rather than seeking cover, massed in the streets and eagerly watched the spectacle. Then the planes turned again to Wiener Neustadt, Graz, Ljubljana, Trieste, and Venice, and safely landed at San Pelagio again; it was 12:40 in the afternoon.

No doubt d'Annunzio insisted on a last roll call of the "Seven Lions of Vienna," as the pilots were called later (he had stipu-lated that the planes carry the insignia of the lion of Venice), and I am certain they had to shout "Eia Eia alala!" D'Annunzio introduced this shout to military ritual (and it was later taken over by the fascists), instead of the barbarian and ill-sounding (especially to a lover of the ancients) "Ip! Ip! Urrah!" It all looked impressively staged, but not all was well with the 87th Squadron. Sarti, after landing near Wiener Neustadt, com-plained about the policies of his superiors, and Aldo Finzi, who, at twenty-six years of age, was one of the oldest of the pilots

and one of d'Annunzio's favorites, left the squadron because of a
conflict with its commander, Masprone. Much decorated for his
courage, he turned up as a legionnaire in d'Annunzio's Free Republic of Fiume, worked closely with Mussolini, who named him
assistant commissioner of aviation in 1923 and undersecretary
of the interior. He tendered his resignation, however, when the
fascists were forced to cover up for their murder of the socialist
Giacomo Matteotti. (In John Krizanc's remarkable play of 1981
about d'Annunzio and his women, Finzi turns up as a fascist
killer with black gloves.) Finzi stayed on as deputy in the fascist
parliament, though, and cultivated his tobacco fields. In 1941 he
was put under police supervision because he had spoken out
against the regime, and a year later was expelled from the fascist
party. He was arrested by the Germans on 24 February 1944 and
killed, as a Jew and a partisan, with 344 others in the Ardentine
caves of Rome.

MANY HUNDREDS of thousands of leaflets, printed on white or
tricolored paper, were carried to Vienna. Some were written by
d'Annunzio, others composed by Ugo Ojetti, a journalist, noted
literary critic, and loyal but not uncritical friend of d'Annunzio's. Fortunately, the poet's text was not the one he had penned
in the earlier stage of planning about the mythical clashes of the
Latin and the barbarian races. It declared now that Austria's
hour was gone, and that the armies of the Entente on the Piave
and the Marne, and the new reserves, including the mighty
Americans, were close to victory. Austria should not any longer

be "dragged along, humiliated, and infected" by Germany. Ojetti was right to say that the wording was rather poetic and untranslatable and would, if translated, sound forced and rather foolish, *goffissimo*. Ojetti himself wanted a well-organized and logical text that would appeal to the tired and hungry Viennese. He chose the shape of a timely political argument of four parts—assumption, countervoice, conclusion, and exhortation—and presented thoughts that spoke to the stomach, to people in long breadlines, weary of the future. Indisputably, he argued, the cause of Austria was lost because of the military might of the Entente (with 1,200,000 Americans now in the field) and its economic power; and while the Allies were not willing to conclude a peace treaty with the present imperial government or with Germany, which had lost all trust, they were ready to negotiate with the people, and especially the liberated nations of Austria-Hungary. The Entente was ready to feed the hungry, offer a peace of freedom, work, and mutual respect, and guarantee the right to property, jobs, professions, and all social laws—only the generals and militarists had to go. He even appealed to the intelligence of the Viennese and asked them why they should go on believing the promises of the Prussian generals. Believing them was like waiting for the famous bread from the Ukraine—everybody could die waiting for it!

It is difficult to guess whether the Viennese mission was a success, or of what kind, but Viennese newspaper reports and comments, both official and unofficial, reveal something about the impressions made by the daring operation, the response of the high command, and the attitude of the Viennese. Local observers believed that there were seven or eight planes, and at four o'clock in the afternoon the number was reduced to six (there were seven); in general, official commentators stressed that it was difficult to warn the population of the raid because the squadron flew at an altitude beyond the range of early detection. Poor Giovanni Sarti, who had to make an emergency landing, was declared to be a demonstration of the precise antiaircraft fire that brought him down. (Actually, only the antiaircraft batteries of Ljubljana, in Slovenia, opened fire against the returning Italians, without results, and the Austrian high command never explained the bungled reports on the Italian incursion and why Austrian pursuit planes were helpless because of clouds or because the Italians flew so high.)

Most of the early identifications were erroneous: many Austrian observers reported a flight of Brandenburg planes (the regular type used by the Austrian air force), but others, by noon, knew that the flight had been initiated by d'Annunzio, and the planes were identified with (belated) expertise. At least two papers, the stubbornly conservative *Reichspost* and the socialist *Arbeiter Zeitung*, suggested in unison that the raid was an amazing "aviatic achievement" that should not be belittled for political reasons. It was an admirable "sporting event" requiring a good deal of pure nerve and physical resistance—especially considering the nearly hurricane-force winds to which the pilots' faces were exposed, in the open cockpits (*Arbeiter Zeitung*). It was a moment in Vienna's war history "wanting to be remembered." But the population did not show any heroic feelings, and a few human-interest stories, involving ordinary citizens, a court musician, a park guardian, or a painter in the fourth district using his opera glasses, suggested, rather, that for a long time they thought the planes were Austrian, until they discovered that they did not have the Iron Cross insignia and were Italian after all.

The "population remained totally calm," the liberal, and middle-class, *Neue Freie Presse* reported. There was no unrest, the newspapers went on to say, because the citizens really thought that the planes were Austrian, on a test flight from the nearby airfield of Aspern, or that it was another government stunt advertising war bonds. The Viennese police had, of course, published a number of directives to be followed in case of an air raid—to stay away from the streets, balconies, and windows. However, people were watching with great interest. Roofs were packed, said the *Arbeiter Zeitung*, and crowds assembled to catch the fluttering leaflets, often coming down en masse in their original paper sleeves. The early editions of the newspapers admonished the people to hand over all leaflets to the police, and not to pass them on (a crime of high treason), but many did read them.

D'Annunzio, who had enjoyed his appearance at the Burgtheater in 1900, had a bad press: his style was said to be "comic" or fustian (*schwülstig*). Ojetti enjoyed more success; at four o'clock in the afternoon an official communiqué of the government press bureau reported—whether it was utter foolishness or a stroke of genius—Ojetti's complete text without cuts, and it was immediately reprinted in full by all the newspapers, right, center, and left. Karl Kraus, merciless satirist and sole contributor to his periodical *Die Fackel*, added a final touch: he quoted a report saying that a plane was seen over Rodaun, a district of elegant villas, and suggested sardonically that it was, of course, d'Annunzio himself who wanted to drop in on Herr von Hofmannsthal, the famous poet, to insist that he reciprocate the visit one day.

Yet d'Annunzio's flight was an immediate sensation in the capitals of the Entente, and he was invited by the British high command to have tea at the London Savoy (he had received the War Cross earlier). It was not explained why he never arrived there. He flew over northern France, only to return to Italy; it was his last flight (September 1918). His declining years at his villa at Gardone, on Lake Garda, were not a soaring swoop among the clouds but rather a time of corrosive accommodation, accepting the support of the fascist state, occasionally criticizing, more often praising Mussolini, and welcoming the Duce for a few grim visits. He was spied on by the local prefect of police, who daily reported to Rome, and by the German Foreign Office, which installed a woman agent among his resident harem, and he wasted his old age on drugs and local prostitutes. It was as if Icarus had voluntarily returned to a gilded cage, and I wonder whether he knew how deep he had fallen.

CHAPTER TWELVE

Aviators at Brescia:
Selective Views

D'ANNUNZIO and the Futurists, who disliked each other, unanimously created the ideological image of the aviator as an ascetic, wiry, and heroic superman easily rising above women and all other terrestrial humanity. Fortunately, the air shows of the historic years 1909–12 attracted remarkable people of different kinds and interests, and confined the goggled superman to fiction. There were sports champions and race drivers like Umberto Cagno or Henri Rougier, who switched from Targa Florio or Monte Carlo cars to planes, set on breaking records and pocketing the prize monies; there were workshop managers and future industrialists like Blériot and Curtiss, who wanted to demonstrate the virtues of their machines, and for whom prize money was welcome as capital to be invested in aeronautics; there were military men with strong technological imaginations, like Calderara; there were noblemen like Barone Leonino da

Zara, who tried to fly without much success; and there were unfortunate amateurs from the provinces who built their planes all
by themselves in their barns. Still others, however enthusiastic,
did not know how to handle their planes and were not well
taught, like Faccioli and Cobianchi. Luigi Barzini was right
when he wrote in the *Corriere della Sera* that his Italian compatriots had underrated the advances made in France, the United
States, and elsewhere, and were largely unprepared to compete
with those who had punctiliously tested their machines and
trained long hours under adverse conditions, and who did not
rely on mere aspiration and bravado.

LOUIS BLÉRIOT: THE MAN WHO ALWAYS CRASHES

After he had crossed the Channel, Louis Blériot attracted huge
crowds to all the air shows in which he participated. Both Kafka
and d'Annunzio, if for different reasons, came to Brescia to see
him fly, or to fly with him. He was an inventive engineer, designer, and producer of airplanes who always wanted to show
what his machines could really do. He was definitely not a
sportsman à la Hubert Latham, cigarette dangling from his
mouth, nor did he possess Glenn Curtiss's infinite cool patience
in trying to minimize all personal risk.

Among his fellow flyers he was, surprisingly enough, known
as *l'homme qui tombe toujours*, the man who always crashes, and
only after the physicians told him, following a particularly
dangerous crash, that he should stop flying because they had

discovered a lesion on his heart was he willing to reduce the frequency of his flights and leave the control to others, especially his friend and disciple Alfred Leblanc.

In spite of what the crowds may have believed, Blériot was not always a man who had easy successes. Before he became an icon of early-twentieth-century flying, he had to sell his châteaulike family home because he had invested too much of his capital in planes nobody was buying. After the 1918 demobilization, he had to diversify, and rather than concentrating on fighter planes, he designed and sold motorcycles, sidecars, little automobiles, called "Whippets" in England, and even furniture. His advancing age was not made easier by the economic crisis of 1929 and by his continuing conflicts with French bureaucracies.

Blériot was born in 1872 at Cambrai, to an old and distinguished Catholic family (Louis XVIII slept in their family mansion on his return from exile), went to school in Amiens and Paris, and, early convinced that in his time science would dominate, entered the École Centrale des Arts et Manufactures. He left it at twenty-three, a qualified engineer ready to establish his own production of automobile headlights of his own invention and later dynamos, batteries, and claxons of all shapes. By 1900 he was a successful businessman, and he married Alicia Védère, eighteen years old, who became the mother of his six children; she was always at his side, and much less pessimistic than he sometimes was. He had built his own *ornithoptère*, a little flying machine that flapped its wings like a bird, joined a study group of the French Aero Club, observed Voisin's first experiments with a glider over the Seine, and for a brief time collaborated with him on a similar contraption that never rose from the lake surface where they experimented with it.

Beginning in 1906, Blériot built a series of monoplanes of various conceptions and shapes, such as the Duck (Blériot V) and the Dragonfly (VI), until he settled on a prototype (VII) capable of many modifications. After various mishaps and crash landings, he was able to fly from Toury to Artenay, fourteen kilometers, in eleven minutes. Yet at the time of the Paris Salon de l'Aéronautique in December 1908, the first of its kind, his situation was bleak; all the major plane designers, including the Wright brothers, were represented there, and though he had developed his advanced Blériot IX, X, and XI planes in the meantime, he did not receive any orders and his money was nearly gone. Fortunately, he won a travel award flying forty-two kilometers from Étampes to Chevilly in mid-July 1909. But he felt under pressure to vie for the £25,000 prize offered by the London *Daily Mail* to the first aviator to cross the Channel, from England to France or the other way around.

Blériot made his decision to compete almost on the spur of the moment, after he had been informed that Hubert Latham had failed (his engine malfunctioned, and Latham was fished out of the water) and against the advice of his physician; he was moving on crutches, since his right foot had been severely burned in a recent mishap. Never mind; he immediately notified the *Daily Mail* that he was ready, and while Latham was frantically trying to have another plane delivered to his camp on the French coast, Blériot, Alicia, and their entourage (later joined by Anzani) went to Calais. His Blériot XI was assembled by two mechanics at a place in the dunes called Barraques, and after a spot of bad weather, he was told in his Calais hotel that the wind had calmed. He made a test flight of eleven minutes close to Latham's camp, and then went up at 4:35 A.M. against some wind gusts, leaving behind the French destroyer *L'Escopette* in the dense morning fog. Blériot landed thirty-six and a half minutes later in a convenient English meadow, scouted in advance by a friend waving a French flag.

Among the first to welcome him were two British customs officers who, after brief questioning, gave him a certificate confirming that he "had not seen on board during the voyage any infectious disease demanding detention of the vessel." Not much later, he was observed on the Dover boardwalk signaling with a white scarf to Alicia on board the destroyer that he was waiting for her to disembark.

Blériot's interview after his flight comes close to being a text of world literature, for it was widely disseminated by the international press and extensively quoted in Max Brod's Berlin article and, more importantly, by d'Annunzio in his novel *Forse que sì, forse que no*. Blériot seems to take great care not to appear as a winged superman as does d'Annunzio's literary imitation, but as a man of moods and weaknesses, resolve and sudden courage. He is grateful to all the members of his team, whom he always mentions by name: his loyal Leblanc; his mechanics, Mamet and Collin; the constructor of the efficient engine (*"Ah! Mon brave Anzani, il ne bronche pas . . ."*) though he does not say that the warm motor oil had an unfortunate tendency to seep out and blow into the aviator's face. Blériot speaks of his flight in terms of quickly changing emotions and potential errors: "for more than ten minutes I was alone, isolated, lost in the midst of the immense sea, and I did not see anything on the horizon or a single ship. The calm, disturbed only by the droning of the motor, attracted me by its dangerous charms, and I was well aware of it." He was directed to the right course by the chance discovery of three ships all going to Dover, *sans doute*, and as soon as he spotted his friend Fontaine signaling the landing point, he felt almost crazy, he said, turned downward, and cut the motor only twenty meters above ground. The undercarriage and the propeller were damaged, but "*Tant pis!* I had crossed La Manche!"

After the magnificent celebrations, dinners, and speeches in London and Paris, Blériot was the most famous aviator of the moment, his feat was celebrated by the media and the masses, and, what meant more to him, orders for his planes poured in, especially the Blériot XI.

At Rheims, a little later, he had to compete for the first time against Glenn Curtiss, and it was Curtiss who won the Gordon Bennett Cup. On Sunday, 29 August, Blériot won the ten-kilometer speed race, but when he went up again a propeller broke, a splinter hit the rudder, the plane went down and completely burned. Blériot barely escaped the fiery crash with contusions and burns, and Curtiss received the *Prix de la Vitesse.* Yet Blériot was tremendously stubborn; in spite of his mishap, he went on to Brescia with two planes of his type XI and one type XII, and was duly received at the Brescia main station by the presiding committee members. His flying performance there lacked force and energy though he tried, and his name was con-

Blériot (right) at Brescia.

spicuously absent from the list of winners. At least his disciple Leblanc was among them.

On the first day he flew with a bandaged shoulder, on the following day he barely avoided a harsh landing, and on 11 Sep-

tember (Kafka and Brod were among the eager spectators) and
12 September he went up a number of times, much admired as
the *geniale aviatore* and recognized by nearly everybody because
of his droopy moustache and his nose, *un po grifagno*, a little
fierce. He ignored d'Annunzio's urgent wish to fly with him, and
by 14 September he was gone, together with most of the other
international aviators. As he left he came close to saying that he
had flown at Brescia *hors concours*, but was prompted by his sin-
cere sympathies for Italy's aviation efforts; he added in an interview that in the future he would abstain from demonstration
flights and concentrate on perfecting the design of his monoplanes.

That was not entirely true; on 26–29 September he was in
Berlin, where he found himself involved in a conflict with the organizers of the show; immediately he proceeded to Cologne,
where he was hosted by Ettore Bugatti, chief manager of the
Deutz automotive works, and once more demonstrated the
virtues of his type XI. On 8 October he went to Frankfurt, won
two awards, and continued with a series of demonstration
flights in Budapest and Vienna, where on 23 October he met
Emperor Franz Joseph I after he had demonstrated his Blériot XI
on the Simmeringer Heide. In December he moved on to Constantinople, where, in spite of strong winds, he took off and
promptly smashed his plane into the roof of a building, his
thirty-second mishap, severely hurting himself. He convalesced
at the French hospital in Constantinople, and later in Vienna.

After the shows of Rheims, Brescia, and Constantinople,
Blériot's life changed greatly. The engineer and workshop man-

ager turned into a captain of industry whose achievements were to form an integral part of French aircraft production and big business. He established three flying schools to sell his models, at Étampes, Mourmelon, and Handon (near London), offered free lessons to buyers of his planes, and was proud of his new disciples, among them Jacques de Lesseps, son of the builder of the Suez Canal and the second aviator, after his teacher, to cross the Channel, as well as Jeanne Herveau, who later became a flight instructor in the United States. In 1915, Blériot built a huge plant at Suresnes (Seine), seat of his Établissement Blériot-Aéronautique, and produced famous fighter planes as well as planes for the advance observation of artillery positions and heavy biplane bombers.

After the war, Blériot shifted his attention to passenger planes used in regular flights from Paris to other European cities; the Paris-London run, for instance, twice daily, at 7:00 A.M. and 12:30 P.M. from Le Bourget, cost three hundred francs, with a free luggage allowance up to fifteen kilograms and delicate wicker chairs for the cabin passengers. Business was not easy in the early 1930s; too many types of airplanes had to be delivered at short notice (while the banks were refusing long-term credit), and the Popular Front government, in the interest of French defense, nationalized the aircraft industry. Blériot, who belonged to a conservative generation of businessmen, did not live to see that day. He died on 1 August 1936 of heart failure, was given a state funeral with full military honors, across a Seine bridge on 5 August, and the nationalization law was passed five days later.

GLENN CURTISS: THE BOY FROM
UPSTATE NEW YORK

To European observers, Glenn Curtiss was a rather obscure American aviator who went to Rheims and within twenty-four hours beat Blériot for the Gordon Bennett Cup, worth five thousand dollars, by a margin of seconds, and won another competition for speed while Blériot crashed. When Curtiss got to Brescia, he was celebrated as the fastest man on earth, or rather in the sky, and as the proverbial American who incarnated everything that the Italian public wanted him to be, a kind of reticent, gangly Gary Cooper who went aloft in an ill-fitting suit. Unlike Blériot, he was decidedly cautious; he walked around with a wetted finger to the wind or was seen sitting in his hangar, calmly reading his *New York Herald-Tribune* (Paris edition), waiting for more propitious weather. He was averse to festive dinners and public speeches (his were usually four lines long and very effective), and totally unwilling to market himself personally. He barely tolerated that, in France, a publicity shot was made of him together with the famous diva Anna Held, and when she asked him for another photo opportunity later in New York, where she had become a star of the Ziegfeld Follies, he glumly told her that once was enough. Money, or rather capital, was of importance to him, and I believe he went to Rheims and Brescia with an eye on the prize money, since his factory was running low on funds. Even before arriving in Europe, he knew that the Wright brothers were suing him, and everybody else flying, for infringement of their patents, and legal procedures went on for the next eight years. He never returned to Europe to fly after 1909, and America was, for better or worse, the scene of his few defeats and many victories.

Glenn Hammond Curtiss was born in 1878, the grandson of a Methodist preacher in the Finger Lakes region of upstate New York. His father did not live long enough for Glenn to show him whether he was a respectable harness salesman or a good-for-nothing given to drink. His mother, of some aesthetic inclinations, soon remarried, moved away, and left the boy to the care of his Hammondsport grandmother, fortunately, for she was a true tower of love, encouragement, and strength. Curtiss left school when he was about fourteen, and never pursued higher education; he first worked as a Western Union telegram delivery boy, racing the other boys on his bike, and for some time for the Eastman Company, in Rochester. Before he was twenty years old, he married Lena Neff, whom he met while picking grapes, and he ran his own bicycle shop. In school he had been good at math, but engineering was in his mind and in his hands; while repairing and selling bicycles, in his spare time he was busy ordering little motors from magazine catalogs, putting them on bikes of his own making. A real hell-rider, he participated in rallies and motorcycle races, and two years after transforming his small shop into the G.H. Curtiss Manufacturing Company in 1904 he won the world speed record for motorcycles at Ormond Beach, Florida (ten miles in eight minutes, fifty-four and two-fifths seconds).

Curtiss was not attracted to flying yet, but a popular balloonist and showman, "Captain" Thomas Scott Baldwin, who was interested in directed balloon flights, heard about his efficient motors and came to Hammondsport to talk to him. In early August 1904, Baldwin made his first directed flight in his California Arrow, powered by a Curtiss motor, and in spring 1907 Curtiss himself went aloft in a dirigible fitted with his four-cylinder motor. Upon landing he declared that flying was delightful, "only there was no place to go."

It took considerable time before Curtiss conceded that flying had a real future, and it was Alexander Graham Bell, inventor of the telephone and a close student of Samuel P. Langley's experiments in 1896 on the Potomac River, who finally converted Curtiss to aviation. Bell had long experimented with man-carrying kites, not particularly intriguing to Curtiss, but again he needed one of the small, efficient motors coming out of Curtiss's Hammondsport shop. Curtiss was, at best, indifferent to Bell's general ideas, and it needed a formal invitation, twenty-five dollars per diem, and free lodging to prompt him to go to Bell's palatial residence in Nova Scotia for further consultation. Everything went exceedingly well. Bell was his most radiant self, and Mrs. Bell, deaf after a bout of typhoid fever, liked Curtiss because he could communicate easily with her, speaking slowly and expressively (his own sister had suffered a severe hearing impairment after meningitis).

In due course—and financed by his wife, who sold off a piece of property—Bell formed an Aerial Experiment Association, gathering around himself four young Canadian and American men (among them, Tom L. Selfridge, the first U.S. Army aviation expert), and Curtiss was promoted to the post of "director of experiments," though usually everybody pitched in and the new contraptions were flown by lot. The Aerial Experiment Association went on, collectively, from kites to gliders and "aerodromes," as Bell called new airplanes—first the Red Wing, then the White Wing, flown by Selfridge and later by Curtiss, and ultimately the famous June Bug, which Curtiss had constructed but which retained the characteristic concave wings of the preceding Aerial Experiment Association models. On 4 July 1908, Curtiss successfully competed in his June Bug for the *Scientific American* trophy, flying more than the one kilometer prescribed, and was awarded the first pilot's license issued by the Aero Club of America.

Curtiss's decision to go to Rheims and Brescia to fly was sudden and perhaps even improvised; Cortlandt Field Bishop, president of the Aero Club of America, who had his own agenda, pushed a great deal, but once Curtiss heard that the Wright brothers had declined the invitation (preferring to do business in Berlin) and that considerable prize monies were to be won, he was ready to go. The trouble was that his plane, a modified version of his Golden Bug, was not yet finished. It was designed for greater efficiency and speed, with a shortened wingspan, stylish tan linen wings, and a powerful eight-cylinder engine capable of delivering, it was hoped, fifty horsepower. Curtiss did not even have a chance to test the plane in Hammondsport; it was shipped while he and his entourage boarded the SS *Savoia*, only to encounter new problems in France because the Paris transport company could not guarantee delivery to Rheims in time. The plane had to be taken apart, and Curtiss carried the parts as somewhat oversized personal luggage on the train to Rheims. It was, however one looked at it, a matter of the American against the European superpilots, his U.S. biplane against the French monoplanes. Blériot, moreover, was widely favored by the people. Bishop was happy to have an American pilot in the race, but when Curtiss was introduced to James Gordon Bennett, who had endowed the prize, and told him that he had come with only one plane (Blériot had five) and a single spare propeller, Bennett, a worldly collector of china and canary bird cages (clearly an early Bruce Chatwin character), looked, it was said, rather distraught.

Curtiss had come for the cup and nothing but the cup, and only after he won it did he try for two other awards. On the seventh day he wanted to fly at the earliest moment allowed by the rules, as long as the good weather lasted. After a brief test flight he had his tank refilled and his propeller changed, and was aloft, roaring up and down the ten-kilometer rectangle, taking sharp curves around the pylons as if he were riding a motorbike. Blériot went up late in the afternoon, possibly too late, and when the results were in, Curtiss had won by 5.6 seconds. All the others were slower, and George Cockburn, a British flyer, had been thrown from his Farman plane. Blériot himself congratulated the winner, and Curtiss was suddenly surrounded by the American ambassadors to Paris and Berlin, the club functionaries, and Mrs. Theodore Roosevelt, who had come with her three children to Europe while her husband was on a hunting trip in Africa. In the evening the American ambassador hosted a five-hundred-person banquet at his Paris residence, and Curtiss, assured that he did not have to make speeches, entered the hall arm in arm with Blériot, the other guest of honor.

After Rheims, Brescia. It was Cortlandt Field Bishop who drove Curtiss and his wife, Lena, in his fashionable car over the mountains and the Gotthard Pass to Italy, while Ted Shriver and Ward Fisher, a longtime friend, went by train, guarding the disassembled plane. They were followed by five hundred American fans and fifteen journalists ready to cheer their champion. On the Italian field, Curtiss was not an obscure pilot anymore; the *Corriere della Sera* declared, even before the show had started, that though Blériot might have been more popular at the moment, Curtiss was certainly more admired.

Curtiss and Blériot had fought their duel, but they both agreed that it was imperative to develop the speed of flying machines, not their capability of reaching high altitudes or staying

A contemporary caricature of Curtiss.

aloft for a prolonged time. They now intended, they added, to increase their speed up to 120 or 150 kilometers per hour. Luigi Barzini, looking at the American plane and pilot, was clearly enchanted; the machine was graceful and sparse, a mere plaything when compared to Blériot's or Voisin's, and yet the small engine unleashed a veritable cyclone when turned on, sending hats flying and raising dust clouds. Curtiss, preparing to win the Grand Prize of Brescia (fifty kilometers) and the flying-start award (one kilometer), was calm and taciturn as usual; he looked like a professor of mathematics, Barzini noted, or the captain of an old ferryboat going on a trip that he had run ten thousand times before. It was characteristic of Curtiss that he decided to compete for the Grand Prize only late in the afternoon, after he had decided that the weather was favorable and would not change. Only at 6:00 P.M. did he go for his first lap of ten kilometers, again taking his turns sharply, as he was wont to do. The only observer in the crowd who was not captivated by his performance was Franz Kafka, who, aware of his own imperfections, bravely wrote "that it was not important to admire perfection" because "it was not necessary to muster any courage to attain perfect achievements." His friend Max Brod rather condescendingly remarked that "some kind of record had been broken," but he at least marveled at the polish of the plane and felt great sympathy for the victorious yet modest aviator walking past the barriers.

At least two instructive American biographies of Curtiss discuss his flight with d'Annunzio as a serious affair, but the local press, as well as Luigi Barzini, who filed a detailed report with his newspaper the next day, was clear about the fact that the hip-and-hop which poor d'Annunzio experienced, crouching on a little wooden board on the lower wing next to the pilot, was hardly a flight at all; there were reasons why d'Annunzio, after his fragmentary experience with Curtiss, went to seek out Calderara, who finally fulfilled his ardent wish. I wonder what d'Annunzio really meant when, as late as 1937, he dedicated a photograph "to the great Curtiss" in French and signed it in English as his "first passenger," in quotation marks. The truth is that Curtiss, unlike Wilbur Wright, did not like to take passengers. He was too cautious, knew a good deal about the instability of planes, and did not want the responsibility. Among the pilots at Brescia, he was the only one who really knew where to start and where to land with precision, said Barzini, and in the case of d'Annunzio, he simply went through the motions.

Curtiss played a similar trick a year later on eighteen-year-old Blanche Scott, who had crossed the American continent in her automobile and was recommended to him as a potential exhibition flyer to the public. It is not clear how much of his personal instruction she enjoyed, but on 2 September 1910 he locked the throttle when he left her alone in the plane, and she found herself suddenly high in the air, whether of her own volition or because the wind had carried the plane aloft. To this day, experts argue whether she was the first American woman to fly, or merely the butt of an elaborate joke. The only passenger that Curtiss ever welcomed on a flight was the famous evangelist Billy Sunday in 1911.

When Curtiss went home from Brescia, he was facing serious

problems, if not financial ruin. The Aerial Experiment Association had been disbanded and he was embroiled in conflicts with new and dubious business partners: the Wright brothers, whose interests were now represented by a powerful corporation, demanded 25 percent on each dollar he was earning. In early 1910 he suggested himself that the future of aviation income was, in addition to prize monies, in "exhibition work" and government contracts. Prize money was important: on 29 May 1910, Curtiss flew his plane 150 miles, following the Hudson River and a railroad train, somewhat slower than his plane, from Albany down to New York, and received the sum of ten thousand dollars, endowed by the *New York World*; not much later he circled over the ocean, starting from Atlantic City, for fifty miles (five thousand dollars). Curtiss was not the only one in the United States who made a good deal of money by training stunt flyers who went on the road and entertained the public by flying under bridges or upside down, went into "death dives" ($1500 a day), or occasionally competed with Harry Houdini over Niagara Falls. I am certain he disliked the appearance of the French Lady (a pilot in drag), who had her garments flutter in the wind.

Yet Curtiss, in spite of his corporate difficulties and the "fancy flying" of his money-making traveling troupes, never gave up his essential commitment. Eventually encouraged by more definite policies of the army and navy, long hesitant to free funds for aviation, he returned to his earlier experiments on Keuka Lake in building an airplane on floats. He concentrated on the construction of what he called a "hydro-aeroplane," at the outset made a successful start in one, taking off from water, and only a week later, in February 1911, the navy ordered its first plane of that kind.

World War I put an end to the Hammondsport idylls; the old workshop was needed to produce engines, and since there was not enough space, in the spring of 1915 Curtiss moved his production site to Buffalo, where nearly ten thousand workers manufactured planes for Great Britain and the United States; he also established a special research and experimental center at Garden City, Long Island, where he took up residence with his family. Even after his retirement in 1920, he kept working on his inventions; the partial list of his aircraft patents and innovations comprises fifty-seven items (excluding those pertaining to motorcycles, sidecars, speedboats, or his late aero-automobile). He died on 23 July 1930, after an appendicitis operation, and the press did not have to remind people that his life spanned the time from man-carrying kites to big flying boats, which, it was projected, would one day cross the Atlantic.

FACCIOLI, DA ZARA, ANZANI, COBIANCHI: ASPIRATIONS, LARGELY UNFULFILLED

Mario Faccioli never showed up at Brescia because his machine, with a wingspan of 6.7 meters and a one-cylinder engine delivering twenty-five horsepower, solely built by his father, Aristide, an engineer in a Turin automobile plant, was not ready to compete. The pilot had to fly standing erect, but the plane did not move for weeks, and when it finally rose a little above the ground, it immediately crashed, to the great chagrin of the family, including Mario's mother, who had sewn the linen covering for the wings. Aristide Faccioli continued to modify the plane, cutting down the wingspan and using a stronger engine, but results, even for some time after Brescia, were modest. Yet on 6 February 1910, d'Annunzio came out to the field near Turin to watch what was going on and inserted a paragraph of praise for the Faccioli family—mother, son, and father—in his Turin version of his set speech about the glories of aviation. Mario received his pilot's certificate in October 1910 and continued to fly his father's planes, but progress again was less than splendid. In Turin in 1911 he competed for the speed prize for biplanes in a pouring rain, and rose in front of the grandstands about fifteen meters above ground, but the propeller broke, destroying the right wing, and the plane was a total loss, though Faccioli once more escaped unhurt.

Barone Leonino da Zara was a youngish landowning gentleman who had a plane built in Turin, but too late for regular inscription in the lists at Brescia; he barely made it, under the fence as it were, and was accepted only after 30 August. His *Aerocurvo* was entirely built by Franz Miller, who also furnished the thirty-horsepower motor; the wings were distinctly curved, like those of a giant bird, and the grand plane was difficult to move. On 12 September, almost at the close of the show, da Zara began to test his engine, and two days later he tried again at least to taxi the plane across the field, without noticeable results. But he did not give up easily; he bought Rougier's recently victorious Voisin plane on the spot, before Rougier had left, and by October he had established a private airfield on his land near

Padua, the first Italian to do so, and invited Calderara's friend
Lieutenant Savoia to teach him how to fly a newly acquired Farman plane, the third he had bought within a short time. The
new airfield was inaugurated on 5 November 1909, but was totally unusable for months because of the strong rains. D'Annunzio duly visited on 28 February 1910, and a famous actor wrote
an enthusiastic letter to the press saying that he had seen
da Zara, wearing a uniform resembling an opera costume from
Il Trovatore, rise to an altitude of six meters! Soon the private
airfield had to be turned over to the military, but da Zara remained as its manager. He was the first Italian pilot to be filmed
in full flight by a cameraman, Ettore Frollo, on 16 January 1911,
and was later heard of as a chairman of the Padua Aeroclub.

Alessandro Anzani (1879–1956) was a motorcycle rider and
an inventive designer, and during the early days of the Brescia
show he was a particular favorite of the Italian public, who enjoyed his "truly youthful enthusiasm," as the local press suggested. Midway through the races it became evident that he
could not contend at all, and after damaging his plane on 12 September, he withdrew from competition. Anzani had left his native Milan in 1900 to go to Paris to work for Buchet's famous
motorcycle factory as both mechanic and racer; six years later he
set up an independent workshop at Courbevoie, giving up racing
and concentrating on design. As early as 1907 he began to develop engines for flying machines, and through the good offices
of Ernest Archdeacon, then president of the French Aero Club,
he met Blériot, who installed his engine of three cylinders,
arranged in the shape of a star, in the machine in which he

crossed the Channel. Anzani was not fully prepared to fly at Brescia; he had logged a few training hours at Châlons-sur-Marne, at the last minute had his Avis biplane put together by two distinguished engineers, but did not have the time to test it, and was lucky not to kill himself. On the opening day he was up, ready and shining, trying repeatedly to get his plane aloft, but in vain, and while he did some flying on 4 and 7 September, he went up only briefly on the twelfth; unfortunately, the propeller detached itself from its shaft and hit the body of the plane, which crashed immediately; it is also possible that the eager mechanics who pushed the plane back into the hangar further damaged its structure. The impulsive Anzani, in a magnanimous gesture, told his flying colleagues to take what they wanted from his wrecked plane, and did not show himself on the field again, or as a pilot elsewhere, ever. He became a successful international industrialist, owning factories in France, England, and Italy, providing efficient engines to Igor Sikorsky (Kiev) and Clyde Cessna (Wichita) among others, and he also produced marine engines, as well as tractors and lawn mowers that purred all over England. The terrestrial reclaimed some of its rights.

Mario Cobianchi, a young balloonist and sportsman, son of a well-to-do Bologna industrialist, went early to the United States, where he admired the Wright brothers. When he returned to Italy he asked the Franz Miller Works in Turin, the first Italian workshop to produce airplanes, to build an *elicoptero* (actually a biplane) according to his own ideas. It was made of steel and fitted with a nine-cylinder motor, providing one hundred horsepower—possibly far too strong, when considering that other winning planes at Brescia were equipped with motors of thirty (Calderara) or at most forty horsepower (Rougier), better proportioned to the fragile structures taken aloft. Together with an attendant engineer and three mechanics, Cobianchi arrived on the field ahead of anybody else, and the committee assigned to him hangar number one. He and his team began to put together the parts of the plane, shipped by car and train, in early July. Something went wrong from the beginning, though, not to speak about his inexperience at the controls; on the day of his first engine test, 7 July, parts of the cooling mechanism came off and, ricocheting off the struts, injured the engineer and a mechanic. On the fourteenth, propeller parts detached themselves, and four days later, trying to land after a brief hop, Cobianchi damaged the plane's undercarriage and frame. On the twenty-sixth, pieces of the propeller came loose again and nearly killed him. He decided that the steel propeller he had been using would not do and that he had to go to Paris immediately to buy a new wooden propeller made in Chauvier's workshop.

Cobianchi was fortunate in his misfortunes; his hangar was the only one not to be devastated by the thunderstorm of 18 August, and when he returned from Paris he declared smoothly that, after all, Blériot had destroyed seven machines before crossing the Channel. During a test on 2 September, the new wooden propeller splintered and Cobianchi went off again to Paris to buy a duplicate, but it did not have enough pull, and the old steel blades had to be put on. The engine noise was so loud that the committee asked him not to run his raucous machine all the time, since the public complained about the hellish noise, and even Blériot worried about Cobianchi's "infernal motor." When the show began, Cobianchi was definitely not ready, and though, on the ninth, the usual noise could be heard from his hangar, little happened. He made a few attempts to roll the plane across the field, but the machine never quite went aloft. It may have dawned on him that he needed another plane and more systematic instruction in flying, and he rushed the plane to his father's factory, rebuilt it as *Cobianchi II*, powered by a reliable Rebus thirty-horsepower motor, and immediately hastened to France to ask Louis Paulhan to be his first flight instructor. In 1910, Cobianchi, among the students at the new Italian training school at Pordenone, made his first real flight, and on 23 November he received his pilot's license. He proudly took his father up in his plane, the first Italian son ever to fly with his father, as he later remembered. At the beginning of the Italian-Turkish War, Cobianchi (together with Cagno, another Brescia failure) joined the newly established Fleet of Volunteer Aviators of Libya. They were shipped to the North African front on 21 November 1911 and, as their final report later said, went on 153 missions, mostly to observe enemy movements, but also on seven flights to bomb Arab trenches. More often, I suspect, the volunteers were active in Italy, doing exhibition flights to inspire people to buy war bonds. (Earlier that year, two American civilian pilots had flown across the Rio Grande with the permission of the rebel Pascual Orozco to monitor military positions around his camp, but were warned that Orozco's own men might fire on them, believing that they were flying for the Mexico City gov-

ernment.) Mario Cobianchi, who once flew over Pisa, imitating
d'Annunzio's superpilot Paolo Tarsis, never became the star aviator he had always wanted to be, but he later turned into an admirable historian of Italian aviation, who movingly camouflaged
his hopes and tears in a nearly five-hundred-page chronicle published in 1943 and showing, day by day and flight by flight, what
had happened on the airfields of Italy.

GUIDO MONCHER: THE AMATEUR
FROM THE PROVINCES

There was something mysterious about Guido Moncher and his
elicoplano, praised as a purely Italian invention and fitted with
a reliable Rebus engine, but he did not fulfill the great hopes
of the press, including the *Corriere della Sera*. Not much later,
Moncher disappeared from the ranks of the aviators, and his late
years are a sad story. Perhaps he did not feel entirely comfortable
among the professionals and engineers, and when his aircraft finally ascended, at least for a brief flight of 150 meters on 10 January 1910, in Milan, he had it flown by his loyal mechanic and
only after it had been substantially modified by none other than
Gianni Caproni, first industrial builder of Italian airplanes.
Moncher, who admired Santos-Dumont and Delagrange, was an
inspired amateur, perhaps the last of the breed who took up flying as a hobby in the course of his many undertakings, commercial and *sportif*, and he left it to others when he recognized they
were going far beyond what he was willing or able to do.

Guido Moncher was born, the only son of modest farmers, in

the Trentino Val de None in 1873. After meager harvests, living was difficult. His father worked on the Innsbruck-Bolzano railroad and, after 1880, emigrated to the United States and perhaps to South America, returning ten years later a rich man, who left his son a fortune of more than one million gulden (we are still on Austrian territory) when he died. Young Moncher first bought an impressive building in Trento and established a kind of gentlemen's department store, Al Buon Mercato, invested capital in a printing business (a newspaper edited by Cesare Battisti, later hanged by the Austrians, was produced there), married Eloide Mayr, an elegant young woman of a well-to-do family (in her diary she dryly noted that 12:15 P.M., 23 June 1904, was the time and date of their first kiss), and, with one of his new in-laws, established the first Trento automobile agency, racing his cars up and down the mountain roads. Flying came next; he went to Paris and Milan to learn what was going on and built his own aircraft, setting his mind on an *elicoplano* to ascend vertically, if at all possible.

Luigi Barzini was particularly interested in Moncher's experiments, but his patience was sorely tried at Brescia because Moncher was secretive about his intentions, and by late August he had not yet arrived on the field. Between 7 and 9 September, Barzini again and again noted in his daily reports that Moncher's hangar was empty, but on 11 September the plane parts finally arrived. A day later the aviator himself started to put them together while his international colleagues were leaving. On 13 September he continued to tinker. Barzini, ignoring a sign that said ENTRY FORBIDDEN, bravely entered the hangar and found Moncher—an affable, somewhat rotund man with a dark monkish beard that covered most of his simple face. Moncher explained to Barzini that his machine, *Eloide I*, was named after his wife and was actually the third he had built, larger than any other aircraft on the field, with a wingspan of thirteen meters, two sets of propellers, a sixty-horsepower engine, and space for a second passenger. Strangely enough, Moncher was not really eager to perform; on 17 September it rained and the soil was too soggy, and on succeeding days Moncher worked on his plane. On 20 September, the last day of the show, the king himself visited Moncher's hangar—Moncher was there with his wife, one of the most stylish women on the field, who always stayed close to him—but the aviator still did not want to go up. He seemed to have made up his mind not to fly, and he promised the king that he would do so at the next possible occasion, in Milan. I suspect he had not tested his "giant of a plane," as the press described it, and did not want to do so in front of the king and the crowds.

It was Franz Kafka who immediately noticed that the Italian flag was flying on Moncher's hangar, though Moncher was a subject of the Austrian emperor. Knowing a good deal about flag-waving from Prague, he immediately wondered about Moncher's intentions. An Italian patriot and activist, Moncher was commander of the Trento volunteer fire brigade and founder of the Trento city band, which he no longer wanted to subsidize when it played the imperial *"Gott erhalte, Gott beschütze"* on Franz Josef's birthday. His pro-Italian activities were known to the Austrian police, and his wife and son were removed from Trento to Innsbruck when the war started in 1914. (I tend to believe that Eloide, a Mayr by birth, was South Tyrolean and did not feel totally alien in the capital of the Tyrol.) Moncher himself served in the Austrian army, driving an officer's car on the eastern front, but when he was discharged and returned to a liberated Italian Trentino, everything had changed. His investments were gone, the new Italian authorities possibly looked askance at a demobilized Austrian soldier, and his former companions and friends suddenly turned against him, questioning his personal honor and integrity. In 1921 he moved with his family to Vienna, where he settled into an unhappy and lonely life. His son changed his name, on the basis of a fascist law of 1926, to the more Italian-sounding Moncherio, and worked for the Italian embassy in Austria. Kafka could have visited the family in Vienna 3, not exactly a plebeian district of the city. He would hardly have recognized Moncher without his beard, with his sad eyes and hollow face, a man tragically disappointed. Moncher died in Vienna on 14 November 1945.

MARIO CALDERARA: A HERO NOBODY WANTED

"At Brescia we have seen only one Italian fly, and that was Mario Calderara," Luigi Barzini wrote in his acute analysis of the air show in the *Corriere della Sera*. The thirty-two-year-old pilot, who was publicly honored by the king, did not easily fit the presumptions of the assembled press corps or, for that matter, the expectations of his superior officers, who had certain ideas about how a student of the elite naval academy at Livorno should behave. They sent him to Brescia because at that moment there was no one else of his training and professional experience among their battalion of "specialists." Lieutenant Calderara did not have an unblemished record (he had been twice arrested for lack of discipline and investigated for behavior unbecoming in a student of the naval academy)—quite apart from his less than soldierly self-irony and his habit of submitting frequent technical memoranda to the naval authorities. Fortunately, they also knew that Calderara had worked for nearly two years with Gabriel Voisin as a designer of airplanes, and had flown at Issy-les-Moulineaux, learning a good deal about French aircraft. He was speedily summoned to Rome when Wilbur Wright brought his Flyer to Centocelle and became his first disciple; after three and a half hours at the controls, Wilbur declared him fully qualified to pilot the American plane and to transfer the results of his training to his fellow officer Umberto Savoia, to whom Wilbur had given a few desultory lessons. By early 1909 he was really the only Italian who knew how to fly the most advanced French and American aircraft, and considering all the Brescia odds, he did wonderfully there.

Mario Calderara was born in Verona in 1877, the oldest son in a family of military traditions and loyalties. His father was an officer of the *Alpini* and later a general, and Mario, after the prescribed classical training, was duly admitted to the naval academy of Livorno to study engineering and to prepare for a career in the navy. He said himself that he was interested in aviation early on; during a training cruise to Ireland, he observed the mysteriously swift flight of seagulls, began to study Lilienthal, and by 1903 he was corresponding with the Wrights. He began

A contemporary caricature of Calderara.

his modest experiments as an Italian follower of the Wright brothers, at least theoretically, by preparing to construct a kite, or rather a glider, that would carry an observer above the deck of a ship, and concentrated on the question of whether a plane, using the force of the wind, could ascend from a ship's prow, or whether it would be more efficient to put it on floats and tow it to gain airspeed.

It was on the aviation training grounds of Centocelle, during the Roman spring of 1909, that the young pilot was praised by the national press and the patriots as Wilbur Wright's first Italian protégé. Wilbur Wright arrived in Rome on 1 April 1909, was received next day in audience by the king (also present were the American ambassador; Major Moris, chief of the Italian special brigade of aviators and not always friendly toward Calderara, to say the least; and Wilbur's European sales representative, Hart O. Berg). A new Wright plane, shipped from Dayton, Ohio, via France to Rome, was put together in a Roman garage, and Calderara had his chance to watch the assembling carefully. Wright went up on 15 April and continued for the following days with a few training flights. Calderara or Savoia was at his side, and he took a few special passengers aloft—Sidney Sonnino, the intrepid chief of government; a Roman countess of Canadian origins; and the minister of the navy, still in charge of all aviation activities. On 22 April, Queen Margherita watched the proceedings, and on 24 April the king appeared with his retinue; while Wilbur was on a training flight with Calderara, he took his hands off the controls (look, Majesty, no hands) to signal to the king that the Italian pilot was in full command of the flight. Four days later, Wilbur left for Paris with his brother and their sister. The Roman Club of Aviators had to pay him 22,000 francs for the plane and another 20,000 for his training Calderara and Savoia. The Italian pilots went on with their flights, attracting more aviators every day. Calderara did not know, I assume, that Wilbur soon wrote to a French colleague that he had left Calderara with "greater misgivings than . . . other pupils, because he was a cigarette fiend and was being badly spoiled by the attention and flattery he was receiving."

Men were usually at the controls of planes, though Harriet Quimby acquired her pilot's license as early as 1911, but on Italian and French fields courageous women early joined the aviators. On the Roman field, Countess Mary Macchi di Cellere, née Kathy Monckton of Canada, went up with Wilbur on 24 April 1909, and Calderara himself invited his beloved countess Emilia

Gamba Ghiselli for a flight in a Wright Flyer on 18 May 1910. (Family myth has it that he proposed to her right there and then, and the countess graciously accepted, telling him that she felt she was in his hands.) But other women also bravely risked aviation adventures in their elaborate hats and long skirts: Léon Delagrange, a sculptor and later a pilot, on a tour of Italy flew at least 250 meters, in Turin on 8 July 1908, with his fellow sculp-

Mario Calderara and his fiancée.

tress Thérèse Peltier, who sported a chic little chapeau for the
occasion and a *jupe-culotte* of her own invention; and on 8 September 1908, Mrs. Hart O. Berg, wife of his European sales
agent, flew with Wilbur Wright in Le Mans, in France. There
were questions of propriety, of course; Mrs. Berg, resolutely
American and brooking no nonsense, bound her skirts together
to prevent their fluttering around her ankles; the cord is clearly
visible in the photograph of the historic moment (preserved at
the Smithsonian), but deleted from a reproduction used for the
daringly modern frontispiece of the official guide to the Brescia
air show; when she moved off the plane, she forgot to untie the
cord and instantly created the aviatory fashion of "hobble
skirts." Observers tell us that Calderara's betrothed followed
her example on her Centocelle flight, and d'Annunzio, always
transfixed by legs and skirts, did not exactly exert his imagination when he tells us in his novel of 1910 that Isabella, intrep-
idly joining Paolo Tarsis in his plane, binds together her skirts
by a ribbon to keep the folds neatly together. She simply did
what other flying women had done before her.

CENTOCELLE AND BRESCIA were days of joy for Calderara
and his friends, if not for nascent Italian aviation, but it is impossible to ignore how fragile these moments were. Calderara
had to witness the near destruction of his Wright Flyer (twice),
survive a dangerous crash in Rome, and suffer minor mishaps on
the Montichiari field. He received spectacular honors because,
unknown to the crowds, he was able to repair the damage effi-

ciently, put a new engine in an unbalanced plane, or simply rise
to the challenge of switching from one plane to another, each
with its own mechanical quirks. He had personally concluded
that Wright planes were more difficult to fly than their French
counterparts; on 6 May 1909 he tested his plane before inviting
a distinguished passenger, but something went wrong with the
horizontal stabilizer or the transmission, as he later believed,
and he suddenly crashed, from an altitude of about ten meters,
and had to be extricated from the wreckage. Found unconscious
with a slight concussion, a bruised face, and injuries to his right
shoulder and his knee, he was immediately rushed to the hospital and later to the villa of Count Cellere, where the Wrights
had stayed, and recuperated there quietly. It took seven weeks to
reconstruct the plane, but since he and his friend Savoia had
watched Wilbur Wright assemble it in April, they knew how to
go about their job, and were assisted by a few soldiers put at
their disposal by the brigade of specialists. On 1 July, Calderara
was at the controls again and successfully tested the capabilities
of the plane, called the Italian Wright forthwith. In parliament
an interpellation was made to ascertain who was responsible for
the damages (the plane was owned by the Roman aviation club).
More trouble unfortunately lay ahead.

The Italian Wright had only just been rebuilt when it had to
be dismantled again to be neatly packed and shipped to Brescia
and from there on a wagon, pulled by an automobile, to the airfield. Calderara and his men, arriving on 16 August, were assigned hangar number three, and Calderara had begun to put
the pieces of his plane together there when, on 18 August, the

famous late-night thunderstorm struck the field and demolished Calderara's hangar, among others, and wrecked his plane (the engine had not been unpacked yet). Indefatigable as ever, the young aviator decided to rebuild the plane immediately, and together with his friend Savoia and seven soldiers, he transported the wreckage to a disused church in Brescia, where, between 21 and 29 August, he once again rebuilt his Wright Flyer and put it back in the hangar, which had also been reconstructed. The trouble was that the Wright engine was not in good shape. Calderara tested the plane twice on 3 September—the second attempt was cut short when the motor began to sputter—and again on the following day. The result of this third test was a near disaster. The plane ascended quickly and the engine responded, but the craft took a sudden slow turn downward; the horizontal stabilizer was dislocated, the lower wing destroyed, and the propeller cut by a wire. Calderara had hoped to substitute an Italian Rebus for the Wright engine, but now, on the eve of the show, the Italian Flyer was out of service. Calderara was happy to use the Ariel Wright plane that Michel Clemenceau had shipped to him from France right after the thunderstorm.

It was not a gift without its own problems, though, and Calderara found himself alternating aircraft, in a difficult if not grotesque situation; he was under time pressure because of the schedule, and unable to test either plane with the new engine, the French Ariel Wright or the rebuilt Italian Flyer, to his full satisfaction, and yet he succeeded against all odds by a remarkable combination of expertise, stamina, and a good sense of improvisation. On 8 September, the first day of the show, he used the Ariel Wright, which quickly spun out of control and crashed in a noise of splintering wood; its center of gravity was not where the pilot had assumed it to be. From then on, he had no other choice but to use the twice-rebuilt Italian Flyer provided with the new Italian Rebus engine; he competed successfully for the Grand Prize of Brescia (and came in second), the International Passenger Transport Prize (first), the Oldofredi Award (one kilometer), and the *Corriere della Sera* Prize (twenty kilometers), and he took d'Annunzio aloft (fortunately in his Italianized American plane, with an Italian engine and a congenial Italian pilot at the controls). On 20 September, Calderara decided to switch back to the French Ariel Wright plane, now repaired, but he promptly crashed again and, for the grand finale in the presence of the king, had to roll out the Italian Flyer once more. He deserved the King's Cup for many reasons.

The navy should have welcomed Calderara home with open arms, but, on the contrary, whether because of a bureaucratic snafu or the ill will of his superior officers, it did not. Nearly everything went wrong after the triumph at Brescia. The results of his Livorno examinations were so bad that they almost dashed his hope for a navy career; a disciplinary commission had to investigate whether or not he had offended a fellow officer; and an airplane he had built in Paris was removed by military order from a Centocelle hangar and nearly destroyed outside. These difficulties did not prevent Calderara from working, with full authorization by the navy, on the prototype of a new seaplane, and though the new plane, the biggest so far, was found sea- and airworthy on 8 June 1912, the navy decided to buy imported Curtiss seaplanes rather than produce its own according to the Calderara model. Disgusted, Calderara asked for and received a suspension of duty and went to England to lecture on his hydroplane inventions (once in the presence of Winston Churchill) and to work for a British aircraft firm. In 1913 he was recalled to navy duty, and participated in the occupation of Albania, though the island on which he landed his troops was alive only with rats and wild dogs. By 1915, when Italy joined the Allies, he directed the defense of Venice against attacking Austrian airplanes, commanded torpedo boats in the Mediterranean, and was ultimately promoted to run the Bolsena training school of hydroaviation, at which Italian and American pilots trained together. One of the American pilots was, much later, among the first American officers to enter liberated Rome in 1944.

While Calderara's younger brother Attilio made his untroubled career as an officer of the air corps (he became a brigadier general), Mario continued, even after World War I, in and out of the navy. After demobilization he tried his hand at inventing a long-lasting lightbulb called "Sperella," definitely not a financial success, and was appointed air attaché at the Italian embassy in Washington, where he served for about two years (1923–25) during the transitional period when the fascists consolidated their power. I prefer to think that he left the diplomatic service a short while after Matteotti was killed by Mussolini's secret police. He did not return home; instead he relied on the support of his American friends and worked for the Pioneer Instrument Company, a division of Bendix Aviation, relocating with his entire family to Paris to manage European sales of American aviation instruments. There is no evidence that he was in touch with antifascist exiles; rather, I believe, his was a careful balancing act in which he tried to guard his independence as an expatriate, without compromising his or his wife's family at home. In 1939 the French government classified him as an enemy alien and he had to leave quickly for Italy. The navy sent him to Fiume (ironically enough, d'Annunzio's mythic port), but for reasons of health and age they discharged him for good. Mario Calderara died quietly on 16 March 1944, without knowing much about the whereabouts of his son Ludovico, himself a Livorno graduate and officer, who, months before, had gone through the front lines south of Rome to reach Italian units that were turning to fight the Germans.

Epilogue

I WENT TO BRESCIA and Montichiari a few times in recent years, walked on dusty country roads, dodging the trucks, and came away from my journeys with many superimposed images that I am reading one against the other. The scene has changed almost before my eyes, and what I saw three years ago was gone yesterday. The core of Brescia holds on to its magnificent past of churches and palaces, though chic boutiques are spreading through the narrow streets, and in Brescia 2, a new district south of the old railway station, faceless chain hotels are going up like mushrooms after rain, and corporate sales meetings are being held everywhere. I drove to Montichiari on the ancient road, through the villages of Castenedolo and Vighizzolo, and admired the majestic line of poplar trees along the road to Ghedi, duly described by d'Annunzio, and I also stopped at the Fascia d'Oro trattoria and strolled around the piazza of Montichiari. There, on the steps of the magnificent cathedral, a tired U.S. Air Force mother rested her feet while her offspring pestered her for another truly Italian ice-cream cone.

Not much is left of the *brughiera*; the roads are lined with small factories, printing presses, food-processing plants, and metal workshops, and where the air show's grandstand once stood, a cement factory, one of many, dominates the fissured grounds. On my first visit, I noticed that across from the trattoria, a group of poetically decrepit houses was still standing, and from one of them many women, their hair protected by kerchiefs, mysteriously emerged and gathered at the nearby bus station. When I looked at where they were coming from, I discovered the shop of a busy hairdresser, no shingle or name announcing his presence. I returned there about three months ago: the houses had been torn down and a huge gray box without windows, another furniture factory, had gone up.

The shapes of the landscape have been radically rearranged by the opening of the Aeroporto Gabriele d'Annunzio (1999) and the construction of ramps, clustered service halls, and new intertwined roads to fit the new airport into the older traffic patterns. The *brughiera* had attracted race-car drivers and aviators since at least 1906 (not to mention the military planners of the Italian air force, the Germans, the Americans, and NATO), and the new airport, almost adjacent to the aerodrome of 1909, has been established on the runways of an older Italian military airfield that ceased to function about twenty years ago. We are, after all, in the middle of one of the most industrialized regions of Italy, which also handles a growing tourism business around

The Fascia d'Oro trattoria in 2001.

Lake Garda. When the Wall fell in Berlin, Germans (always pre-
dominant among the Garda tourists) from both the east and
west of a unified country came to the lake region; the nearby
airfield of Verona has doubled its passenger volume in the last
four years. The corporation that runs an entire group of local
airports and the appropriate chambers of commerce celebrate

d'Annunzio as the patron-poet of the new airport, in the most effective PR manner, but I wonder whether another choice would not have been more appropriate. True, Verona Airport is named after Catullus, the Latin poet of love, yet, going back to the actual events of the air show of 1909, it would have been fairer to name the renewed airfield after Mario Calderara.

I walked in the departure hall of the Gabriele d'Annunzio Airport while Ryan Air and Air Dolomiti announced their international flights to London and Frankfurt, and yet the events that happened ninety years ago were more immediate to my mind than the sights and sounds of the present, and I thought of the hopes and disappointments of the Brescia aviators who could not see beyond their moment in time. The air show of Brescia, curiously enough, presented much of the then current airplane technology but also something of the present. The fact that so many Italian planes did not start or did not go aloft in itself revealed that, compared with French and American designs, Italian design was still too close to the hapless *ornithoptère* (of the flapping-wing design) or the monstrous *elicoptero*, not to mention Faccioli's triplane, in which the pilot stood upright, like Lilienthal in his gliders in the last years of the nineteenth century. It was almost inevitable that Blériot's, Voisin's, and Wright's planes won the races and that Italy's homespun contraptions could not compete with the technologically fittest. It began to be clear that industrial, or near-industrial, production, careful testing, and perfect training were to prevail in the future.

The original European airfields were established on military exercise grounds on which infantry or cavalry trained, and the first real aerodrome, that of Bétheny near Rheims, was built for people who wanted to attend fashionable races—only the horses and jockeys were planes and pilots. Brescia did not differ. Most people came to see sport, spectacle, or circus, though stunt flying was more consistently developed in the United States; and when planes came to ascend more easily, made their expected turns, or even broke records, people and pilots wanted something more.

The years 1909–12 were the high season for air shows, including those in eastern and southeastern Europe, and yet attention began to shift from "meets" to "raids," or dazzling long-distance flights. They were nothing radically new; dirigible balloons had long tried, sometimes quite successfully, and Henry Farman's flight from Châlons-sur-Marne to Rheims (30 October 1908), followed the next day by Blériot's flight from Toury to Artenay, as well as his crossing of the Channel, were "raids" in early shapes. They were followed by the circuit of eastern France (1910), the Paris-Rome competition (May 1911), the Bologna-Venice-Rimini-Bologna race of 1911, and Roland Garros's daring flight from France to the coast of Tunis (1912). Rather than air shows, people now gathered to watch the start or finish of a sensational raid.

Increasingly, flying was of interest to industrial designers, engineers, and military planners. Many new aviators were certified (by 1910 there may have been 450), and fatal incidents multiplied. The year of the Brescia air show was bad enough: Tom L. Selfridge (U.S. Army) was killed in America and the daring

Eugène Lefebvre and Captain Ferber in France, all of them true pioneers. In 1910 the number of deaths rose catastrophically, among them Léon Delagrange (4 January), who had taken flying from France to Italy; Charles Wächter in Rheims; Charles Rolls at Bournemouth; Georges Chaves, who flew over the Alps and crashed at Domodossola (27 September); Ralph Johnston in the United States; and in the last four days of December alone, four aviators in France and in the United States fell to their deaths. The Austrian Lieutenant Colonel Hermann Hoernes, who kept account of the accidents, noted in his grim chronicle that, in 1910, fifteen balloonists and twenty-eight pilots died in fatal accidents.

The air show of Brescia was an almost Arcadian affair. There were a number of crashes, but aviators walked away from their damaged planes briskly or sadly, and the unfortunate peasant who fell off the overcrowded new tram from Montichiari to Brescia hurt himself more than any of the pilots. Records were few and rarely acknowledged by the French; Henri Rougier rose to 198.5 meters, or nearly 650 feet, on the last day, but within three weeks the Comte de Lambert, a disciple of Wilbur Wright, went up 300 meters, and on 10 January 1910, Hubert Latham reached an altitude of one kilometer at Châlons-sur-Marne. Gentlemen in their Sunday best and ladies in their elaborate dresses milled around in the less expensive enclosure, others were having their Pellegrino at the grandstand restaurant where Puccini held forth.

Watching planes ascending and landing for the first time in his life, Franz Kafka had dim forebodings about humanity be-

The monument to the aviation pioneers of 1909.

coming too mobile and possibly alienating itself from its traditional homes and beliefs, and d'Annunzio, the grand actor in the drama of his own life, came to add the role of the pilot-warrior to his repertory. In the *Frankfurter Zeitung* on 21 August 1909, as if celebrating the finale of the show, Carl Vollmöller, a pilot and poet himself, wrote, in an essay titled "Aviatica," that the history of aviation had been so far "a triumph of dilettantism" (not entirely missing his mark), and he rightly believed that the future would come to prefer light and efficiently constructed planes. It was a completely different question whether, as he asserted, aviation would have its revenge on the new militarism because people were tired of war, and whether aviators would bring together states and societies more closely. (I hope he did not change his mind when translating d'Annunizo's novel two years later.) At the time of Brescia, all possibilities seemed to be open, and the air show, so contradictory and such a muddle of aspiration, courage, and disappointment, may have been the last luminous moment of a strange innocence, something rare that should not be forgotten.

BIBLIOGRAPHICAL NOTES

GENERAL ABBREVIATIONS

In the course of my readings I found three volumes truly indispensable, each essential and pioneering in its own way.

COB = Mario Cobianchi, *Pionieri dell'aviazione in Italia* (Rome, 1943)

ING = Felix Philipp Ingold, *Literatur und Aviatik: Europäische Flugdichtung 1909–1927* (Basel, 1978)

WOH = Robert Wohl, *A Passion for Wings: Aviation and the Western Imagination* (New Haven, 1994)

I also consulted the appropriate issues of the local, provincial, and national Italian newspapers, including:

SB = *La Sentinella Bresciana*

PdB = *La Provincia di Brescia*

CdS = *Corriere della Sera* (Milan)

In the first days of September 1909, the organizing committee of the Brescia air show published an official program that included many illustrations and articles about aviation, *Il circuito aereo di Brescia. Guida ufficiale* (Milan, 1909). A Milan printer issued a competing (if unapproved) volume, *Il volo degli uomini; Teoria, storia dell'aviazione e guida del I. circuito aereo di Brescia* (Milan, 1909). In subsequent years, civic institutions of the region and a Montichiari publisher marketed a number of commemorative volumes, among them *Rotary Club di Brescia. Cinquantenario del I. Circuito Aereo* (Brescia-Montichiari, 1959), the first in Italy to mention Franz Kafka's presence again, 33–35. *La nascita dell'aviazione italiana. Il I. Circuito aereo di Brescia nella brughiera di Montichiari* (Zanetti editore, Montichiari, 1979); *Oggi si vola. Brughiera di Montichiari. A cura di Biblioteca Comunale* (Montichiari, 1981); and, most recently, the magnificent chamber of commerce Festschrift, *Aeroporto Gabriele d'Annunzio—Montichiari/Brescia. A cura di Annamaria Andreoli* (Brescia, 1999).

CHAPTER 1. THREE FRIENDS, VACATIONING

Max Brod

On Riva at the turn of the century: *Österreich-Ungarn, nebst Bosnia, Herzegowina, etc.*, by Karl Bädeker (Leipzig, 1907), 215–19. Autobiographical writings: *Streitbares Leben* (Munich, 1960) and *Der Prager Kreis* (Stuttgart, 1966). On Brod: Berndt W. Wessling, *Max Brod* (Stuttgart, 1969), and Margarita Pazi, *Max Brod* (Bonn, 1970), as well as Margarita Pazi, ed., *Max Brod: Zu seinen literarischen und philosophischen Schriften* (New York, 1987). Brod's views of his friend, *Über Franz Kafka* (Frankfurt, 1974), comprise three volumes of Brod's biographical and interpretive writings about Kafka.

Franz Kafka

Personal documents: *Tagebücher 1910–1923*, volume 7 of *Gesamtausgabe* (Frankfurt, 1976); *Briefe 1902–1924* (Frankfurt, 1975); Erich Heller and Jürgen Born, eds., *Briefe an Felice und andere Korrespondenz aus der Verlobungszeit*

(Frankfurt, 1976). "Der Jäger Gracchus," in Max Brod and Hans Joachim Schöps, eds., *Beim Bau der chinesischen Mauer* (Berlin, 1931), 43–50; see also commentary by Hartmut Binder in *Jahrbuch der deutschen Schillergesellschaft* 15 (1971), 375–440. Useful biographical studies: Klaus Wagenbach, *Franz Kafka: Eine Biographie seiner Jugend* (Berne, 1958), and Ernst Pawel, *The Nightmare of Reason: A Life of Franz Kafka* (New York, 1984). Important monographical studies: Elias Canetti, *Der andere Prozess: Kafka's Briefe an Felice* (Munich, 1969); Giuliani Baioni, *Kafka: Letteratura ed ebraismo* (Parma, 1984); Ritchie Robertson, *Judaism, Politics, and Literature* (Oxford, 1985); Mark K. Anderson, ed., *Reading Kafka: Prague, Politics, and the Fin de Siècle* (New York, 1990); and Sander L. Gilman, *Franz Kafka: The Jewish Patient* (New York, 1995). See also Hartmut Binder, ed., *Kafka-Handbuch*, 2 vols. (Stuttgart, 1979), especially I, 4, and II, C, aa–dd, by James Rolleston, on Kafka's early prose. W. G. Sebald's "Dr. K. takes the waters at Riva," in *Vertigo*, translated by Michael Hulse (New York, 1999), 139–68, oscillates between fiction and document (original German, *Schwindel Gefühle* [1999]).

Otto Brod

Jürgen Sehrke, *Böhmische Dörfer: Wanderungen durch eine verlorene literarische Landschaft* (Vienna/Hamburg, 1987), 387–88.

CHAPTER 2. INTERLUDES

The International Car Races at Brescia

Albino Miceli, *Storia del circuito automobilistico di Brescia Montichiari* (Brescia, n.d.), 51–55. Also, *Il volo degli uomini*, 51–55, and the *automobilismo* entry in Antonio Fappani, ed., *Enciclopedia Bresciana* (Brescia, 1993), I, 65–66.

From Icarus to Brescia: D'Annunzio's History of Aviation

The basic texts are d'Annunzio's novel *Forse che sì, forse che no* (Milan, 1910),

66–70, and his poems *L'ala sul mare*, in Annamaria Andreoli and Niva Loren-zini, eds., *Versi di gloria e di amore* (Milan, 1984), II, 579, and "Ditirambo IV," II, 581–98; there is excellent commentary at II, 1258–63. Important: ING, 28–49.

The Rheims Aviation Week

Henri-Georges Laignier, *Le livre d'or de la grande semaine* (Paris, 1909), and *L'aviation triomphante: Le Bilan de 1909* (Paris, 1910), which has a day-by-day account, with documents from the French press. Also: WOH, 100–109.

CHAPTER 3. THE ORGANIZATION OF THE BRESCIA *CIRCUITO*

The names of committee members can be found in the *Guida ufficiale*, 163–64, and the biographies of the principal organizers in the *Enciclopedia Bre-sciana*, the entry on Oldofredi, X, 366–67; on Orefici, XI, 94–95; and on Mercanti, IX, 105–6. The choice of the *brughiera* as a location is discussed by Arnaldo Fraccaroli in "La campagna dei voli" in the *Guida ufficiale*, 24–34, and in *Il volo degli uomini*, 55–58. COB, 20–23, is informative about early discussions and the visit of an official French delegation to inspect the air-field. About rules and signals, see the *Guida ufficiale*, 129–43 and 177–81; also *Il volo degli uomini*, 68–73. Reports about the devastating thunderstorm can be found in the local press, e.g., PdB, 20 August and 3 September, and SB, 21 and 22 August.

CHAPTER 4. THE EVENTS OF THE AIR SHOW: A CHRONICLE

I rely on the daily reports in SB, PdB, and on the articles in CdS written by Luigi Barzini, as well as on COB, 23–32; WOH, 111–15; and ING, 25–27.

Later publications are listed in the general section at the beginning of the bibliographical notes.

CHAPTER 5. A NEW SENSATION: *ZODIAC III*

In addition to the publications listed in the general section, I depend on the reports in PdB, 14–17 September, and in SB for the same days. Speculations about the presence or absence of the Italian military dirigible *I bis* in PdB, 5 September, and in CdS, 11 September. Luigi Barzini's "Due Ore in Dirigibile," in CdS, 17 September 1909.

CHAPTER 6. THE GRAND FINALE

Reports in the newspapers listed above, 19–22 September. Moncher: see Memmo Caporilli, *Guido Moncher: Trentino costruttore del primo elicoplano italiano* (Trento, 1992), especially 63–66 (photographs), and Luigi Barzini's reports in CdS, 43–49. The official results: COB, 31–32. The unveiling of the Zanardelli monument and the speeches: PdB, 18 and 21 September.

CHAPTER 7. PUCCINI AT THE RESTAURANT

Of the rich Puccini literature, I used Mosco Carner's and Howard Greenfield's biographies (London, 1958, and New York, 1980, respectively); the letters edited by Vincent Julian Seligman (London, 1938), and Ernst Krause, *Beschreibung eines Welterfolges* (Cologne, 1985).

CHAPTER 8. KAFKA AND THE "AIR DOGS"

Kafka's report on Brescia: conveniently reprinted in Max Brod/Franz Kafka, *Eine Freundschaft: Reiseaufzeichnungen* (Frankfurt, 1987), 17–26; excellent commentary, 268–69. Paul Wiegler, "Der Pindar des Flugfeldes," *Neue Rundschau* 21 (1910), 1620–23. First discussion of Kafka's report: ING, 19–37; see also Hartmut Binder, *Kafka-Handbuch*, II, 248–49. Kafka's prose pieces and fragments can be found in *Erzählungen* (Frankfurt/New York, 1935–46): "Der Kaufmann," 35–37; "Kinder auf der Landstrasse," 25–28; "Ein Landarzt," 146–53; and in *Hochzeitsvorbereitungen auf dem Lande*, 7–38, the Egyptian fragment, 69, and the aphorism about flying/limping people, 272. See also Max Brod and (later) Ludwig Dietz, eds., *Beschreibung eines Kampfes: Die zwei Fassungen* (Frankfurt, 1969), and Max Brod, ed., and Franz Kafka, *Gesammelte Schriften* (New York, 1946), 5, "Der Kübelreiter," 124–26, and "Forschungen eines Hundes," 233–78. Commentaries on Kafka's prose: Ingeborg Henel, in Binder's *Kafka-Handbuch*, II, 220–27, and Jost Schillemeit's commentary on "Forschungen eines Hundes" in *Kafka-Handbuch*, II, 391–402. Important: K. H. Fingerhut, *Die Funktion der Tierfiguren im Werke Franz Kafkas* (Bonn, 1969).

CHAPTER 9. MAX BROD CHANGES HIS MIND

Brod's article on Blériot is in *Die Gegenwart* 37, 676–77. "Die Flugwoche in Brescia," in Brod/Kafka, *Eine Freundschaft: Reiseaufzeichnungen* (Frankfurt, 1987), 9–16; and the commentary, 267–68. Brod's autobiographical writings, strongly self-interpretive, are found in *Streitbares Leben* (Munich, 1960) and *Der Prager Kreis* (Stuttgart, 1966). On Brod, see Margarita Pazi, and B. W. Wessling, section 1. The fiction includes *Schloss Nornepygge* (Berlin, 1908), *Ein tschechisches Dienstmädchen* (Berlin, 1909), *Jüdinnen* (Leipzig, 1911), and *Arnold Beer: Das Schicksal eines Juden* (Berlin, 1910). Kafka's notes on *Jüdinnen* are in his *Tagebücher 1910–1923*, edited by Max Brod (New York, 1948), 52–54. On early Czech aviation, see Zdeněk Šmoldas, *Průkopníci českého letectví* (Hradec Kralové, 1984), with illustrations and an early portrait of Božena Láglerová.

CHAPTER 10. A DIRGE FOR OTTO BROD

Unfortunately, very little is known about the life and achievements of Max Brod's brother, though Max wrote a good deal about Otto in his autobiographies, especially in *Der Prager Kreis*, 158–167, and his novels *Der Sommer, den man zurückwünscht* (Munich, 1952) and *Die Frau, nach der man sich sehnt* (Vienna, 1927), in the figure of a young boy and Austrian army officer. Otto Brod's own novel *Die Berauschten* was published by E. P. Tal in Vienna, and Max asserts that Otto collaborated with him on the novel *Abenteuer in Japan* (Amsterdam, 1938). See Jürgen Serke, *Böhmische Dörfer: Wanderungen durch eine verlorene literarische Landschaft* (Vienna/Hamburg, 1987), 387–88. Traces of Otto in Theresienstadt are found in H. G. Adler, *Theresienstadt: Das Antlitz einer Zwangsgemeinschaft* (Tübingen, 1960, 2d ed.), 443, and elsewhere, and in the new *Yearbooks* of research about Terezín, and its cultural activities, e.g., 1998, 232–50; 1999, 251–61; and 2000, 123–39, all published by Academia, Prague. Max Brod's poems about his brother are in *Gesang einer Giftschlange* (Munich, 1966), 27–28, 29–30.

CHAPTER 11. D'ANNUNZIO: POET AND AVIATOR

Each generation reads its own biographies of d'Annunzio; I relied on Paolo Alatri, *D'Annunzio e il suo tempo* (Genoa, 1992); John Woodhouse, *Gabriele d'Annunzio: Defiant Archangel* (Oxford, 1998), equally illuminating and fair in matters literary and political; and on Paolo Valesio's *Gabriele d'Annunzio: The Dark Flame* (New Haven, 1992), as well as on Annamaria Andreoli's magisterial *Vivere inimitabile: Gabriele d'Annunzio* (Milan, 2000). I also consulted Tom Antongini, *Quarant'anni con d'Annunzio* (Milan, 1957); Guglielmo Gatti, *Le donne nella vita e nell'arte di Gabriele d'Annunzio* (Modena, 1961); Annamaria Andreoli, *Album d'Annunzio*, with an iconography assembled by Eileen Romano (Milan, 1990); and Renzo de Felice, *D'Annunzio politico 1918–1928* (Rome, 1978).

I quote, or translate, from d'Annunzio's *Forse che sì, forse che no* (Milan, 1910); *Notturno* (Milan, 1921); *Taccuini*, edited by Enrica Bianchetti and Roberto Forcella (Milan, 1965); and *Solus ad solam* (Milan, 1939).

On the poet and fast cars: C. A. Traversi, *Gabriele d'Annunzio: Curriculum vitae 1883–1910* (Rome, 1932), I, 145–53. From Centocelle to Brescia: D'Annunzio's letters to Mario Calderara, in Lodovico Calderara and Attilio Marchetti, *Mario Calderara: Aviatore e inventore* (Florence, 1999), 139–40. D' Annunzio's letters to Donatella on arriving at Brescia: Pierre Pascal, ed., *Le livre secret de Gabriele d'Annunzio et de Donatella* (Padua, 1947), I, 112–13. The confusion surrounding the poet's first flight(s) can be reduced by going back to contemporary press reports, e.g., SB, 13 September, and Barzini's articles in CdS, 11 and 13 September. On *"velivolo,"* see *Vocabolario della Lingua italiana* (Rome 1994), IV, 1124–25, and Mario Vecchioni, *Dizionario delle immagini dannunziane* (Pescara, 1974), 1419.

An important textual analysis of d'Annunzio, Blériot, and aviation questions: ING, 19–49 and 91–94. Saverio Laredo de Mendoza compiled an inclusive source book, *Gabriele d'Annunzio aviatore di guerra* (Milan, 1931), with the lectures on aviation, 69–85, and the memorandum on effective bombing, 157–68. Also, *La guerra d'Annunzio* (Udine, 2001), 259–89, has a good collection of photographs, including a portrait of Aldo Finzi, 256. A new collection of research essays, Gregory Alegi, ed., *Il volo per Vienna* (Milan, 1993), has, of special importance, Eleonora Ledda, "D'Annunzio e il volo tra mito e la realtà," 179–85, and Bernhard Tötschinger, "Il volo di d'Annunzio visto da Vienna," registering Austrian military responses to the Italian incursion of Vienna airspace.

Aldo Finzi appears as a dramatic figure in *Tamara*, a remarkable play by the Canadian writer John Krizanc (Toronto, 1989), which has been performed in Toronto, New York, and elsewhere. I am very thankful to my Austrian translator, Andrea Marenzeller, whom I asked to comb through the Vienna newspapers of August 1918 (totally neglected by Italian historians);

I quote, for instance, from the *Reichspost*, *Arbeiter Zeitung*, and *Neue Freie Presse* of 9 and 10 August; Ugo Ojetti's text was published by the *Neues Wiener Tagblatt* on 10 August 1918. Sarti's emergency landing was covered by the local press, e.g., the *Wiener-Neustädter Nachrichten* (17 August) and even the *Steinfelder Nachrichten* (23 August), all loyally preserved by town librarians, to whom I owe a particular debt of gratitude.

CHAPTER 12. AVIATORS AT BRESCIA: SELECTIVE VIEWS

Blériot

Jacques Mortan, *La vie des hommes illustres de l'aviation* (Paris, 1926). Emmanuel Chadeau, *De Blériot a Dassault: L'industrie aeronautique de France* (Paris, 1987). Louis Blériot, *Blériot: L'envoi du XXe siècle* (Paris, 1999), a unique and massive volume by the aviator's grandson, to be followed by a companion volume on Blériot as industrialist.

Curtiss

Clara Studer, *Barn Storming Yankee: The Life of Glenn Curtiss* (New York, 1937). Alden Hatch, *Glenn Curtiss: Pioneer of Naval Aviation* (New York, 1942). Most important, C. R. Roseberry, *Glenn Curtiss: Pioneer of Flight* (Syracuse, 1991), on Brescia, 200–203.

Faccioli, da Zara, Anzani, Cobianchi

Faccioli: COB, 14, 53–54, 69–70, and elsewhere; da Zara: COB, 26–27, 30, 46, and elsewhere; Anzani: COB, 25–26, 28–30, 39–40, and Anzani Web site; Cobianchi: COB; Moncher: Memmo Caporilli, *Guido Moncher: Trentino costruttore del primo elicoplano italiano* (Trento, 1992), richly documented, but a little reticent about the twists and turns of Moncher's later life.

Calderara

The recent publication of Ludovico Calderara's admirable biography of his father, *Mario Calderara: Aviatore e Inventore* (Florence, 1999), supersedes all previous articles and books about early Italian aviation, including Clemente Prepositi's *La storia dell'aviazione* (Florence, 1931), I. General Attilio Marchetti has contributed the ample notes and commentaries, constituting a complete history of the beginnings of Italian aviation.

EPILOGUE

Hermann Hörnes, *Buch des Fluges* (Vienna, 1911–12), 3 vols. Carl Vollmöller, "Aviatica," *Frankfurter Zeitung*, 21 August 1909. Annamaria Andreoli, ed., *Aeroporto Gabriele d'Annunzio: Montichiari/Brescia 1909–1999* (Brescia, 1999).

INDEX

Page numbers in *italics* refer to illustrations.

ILLUSTRATION CREDITS

ii The official poster of the Brescia Air Show, first published in 1909. Original postcard from the archive of Peter Demetz.

19 Kafka and his friends in the Viennese Prater, reprinted with the permission of Klaus Wagenbach Verlag, Berlin.

46 Caricatures of four members of the air show's organizing committee, from the *Guida ufficiale*, 1909.

51 The location of the 1909 Brescia airport, from "Il volo degli uomini" in *Teoria, storia dell'aviatione e guida del primo circuito di Brescia*, 1909.

55 A simplified sketch of the Brescia airfield, from the *Guida ufficiale*, 1909.

56 An artist's view of the Brescia airfield, from the *Guida ufficiale*, 1909.

67 A hangar at Montichiari, from the collection of Ferlucci Santo (Brescia), reprinted with permission.

71 The title page of the *Guida ufficiale*, 1909.

97 Rebus Motor advertisement, from *Teoria, storia dell'aviatione e guida del primo circuito di Brescia*, 1909.

114 Kafka's newspaper article in *Bohemia*, reprinted from Peter Demetz, ed., *Franz Kafka a Praha* (Prague, 1947).

153 Countess Giuseppina Mancini, reprinted with the permission of the D'Annunzio Foundation.

159 Curtiss and d'Annunzio, reprinted with the permission of the D'Annunzio Foundation.

178 The projected flight plan of d'Annunzio's raid on Vienna, reprinted with the permission of the D'Annunzio Foundation.

192 Blériot at Brescia, reprinted with the permission of the D'Annunzio Foundation.

200 A contemporary caricature of Curtiss, from the *Guida ufficiale*, 1909.

215 A contemporary caricature of Calderara, from the *Guida ufficiale*, 1909.

217 Mario Calderara and his fiancée, from Lodovico Calderara and Attilio Marchetti, *Mario Calderara: Aviatore e Inventore* (LoGisma Editore, Florence, 1999). Reprinted with the permission of Lodovico Calderara.

226 The Fascia d'Oro trattoria as it appears today, from the archives of Paola Gambarota. Reprinted with permission.

230 Monument to the aviation pioneers of 1909, from the archives of Paola Gambarota. Reprinted with permission.